Representations of Sport

This ground-breaking interdisciplinary collection brings together leading international scholars working across the humanities and social sciences to examine ways in which representations of sports coaching in narrative and documentary cinema can shape and inform sporting instruction. The central premise of the volume is that films featuring sports coaches potentially reflect, reinforce or contest how their audiences comprehend the world of coaching. Despite the growing interest in theories of coaching and in the study of the sports film as a genre, specific analyses of filmic depictions of sports coaches are still rare despite coaches often having a central role as figures shaping the values, social situation and cultural expectations of the athletes they train. By way of a series of enlightening and original studies, this volume redresses the relative neglect afforded to sports coaching in film and simultaneously highlights the immense value that research in this emerging field has for sporting performance and social justice.

This book was originally published as a special issue of the journal *Sports Coaching Review*.

Katharina Bonzel is a Visiting Fellow in Screen Studies at the Australian National University, Australia, and is currently writing a book about the representation of national identity in sports films.

Nicholas Chare is Associate Professor of Modern Art in the Department of History of Art and Film Studies at the Université de Montréal, Canada. He is the author of *Sportswomen in Cinema: Film and the Frailty Myth* (2015).

Representations of Sports Coaches in Film

Looking to Win

Edited by
Katharina Bonzel and Nicholas Chare

Routledge
Taylor & Francis Group

LONDON AND NEW YORK

First published 2017 by Routledge

2 Park Square, Milton Park, Abingdon, Oxfordshire OX14 4RN
52 Vanderbilt Avenue, New York, NY 10017

Routledge is an imprint of the Taylor & Francis Group, an informa business

First issued in paperback 2018

British Library Cataloguing in Publication Data
A catalogue record for this book is available from the British Library

ISBN 13: 978-1-138-63627-9 (hbk)
ISBN 13: 978-0-367-13955-1 (pbk)

Typeset in Minion Pro
by diacriTech, Chennai

Publisher's Note
The publisher accepts responsibility for any inconsistencies that may have arisen
during the conversion of this book from journal articles to book chapters, namely
the possible inclusion of journal terminology.

Disclaimer
Every effort has been made to contact copyright holders for their permission to
reprint material in this book. The publishers would be grateful to hear from any
copyright holder who is not here acknowledged and will undertake to rectify any
errors or omissions in future editions of this book.

MIX
Paper from
responsible sources
FSC FSC™ C013985
www.fsc.org

Printed in the United Kingdom
by Henry Ling Limited

Contents

Citation Information   vii
Notes on Contributors   ix

1 Introduction: Sports coaching on film   1
  Katharina Bonzel and Nicholas Chare

2 Configuring Irishness through coaching films: *Peil* (1962) and *Christy Ring*
  (1964)   14
  Seán Crosson

3 "I love you guys": *Hoosiers* as a model for transformational and limited
  transactional coaching   29
  Bryan Mead and Jason Mead

4 The traditional, the ideal and the unexplored: sport coaches' social identity
  constructs in film   41
  Sue Jolly and John Lyle

5 Mind the gap: female coaches in Hollywood sports films   54
  Katharina Bonzel

6 Sound coaching: tending to the heard in American football films   70
  Nicholas Chare

7 Film depictions of emotionally abusive coach–athlete interactions   87
  Gretchen Kerr, Ashley Stirling and Ahad Bandealy

8 Too hot to handle? A social semiotic analysis of touching in "*Bend it like
  Beckham*"   102
  Dean Garratt and Heather Piper

CONTENTS

9 'We're In This Together:' neoliberalism and the disruption of the
coach/athlete hierarchy in CrossFit   116
Leslie Heywood

Index   131

Citation Information

The chapters in this book were originally published in the *Sports Coaching Review*, volume 5, issue 1 (May 2016). When citing this material, please use the original page numbering for each article, as follows:

Chapter 1
Introduction: Sports coaching on film
Katharina Bonzel and Nicholas Chare
Sports Coaching Review, volume 5, issue 1 (May 2016) pp. 1–13

Chapter 2
Configuring Irishness through coaching films: Peil *(1962) and* Christy Ring *(1964)*
Seán Crosson
Sports Coaching Review, volume 5, issue 1 (May 2016) pp. 14–28

Chapter 3
"I love you guys": Hoosiers *as a model for transformational and limited transactional coaching*
Bryan Mead and Jason Mead
Sports Coaching Review, volume 5, issue 1 (May 2016) pp. 29–40

Chapter 4
The traditional, the ideal and the unexplored: sport coaches' social identity constructs in film
Sue Jolly and John Lyle
Sports Coaching Review, volume 5, issue 1 (May 2016) pp. 41–53

Chapter 5
Mind the gap: female coaches in Hollywood sports films
Katharina Bonzel
Sports Coaching Review, volume 5, issue 1 (May 2016) pp. 54–69

Chapter 6
Sound coaching: tending to the heard in American football films
Nicholas Chare
Sports Coaching Review, volume 5, issue 1 (May 2016) pp. 70–86

Chapter 7
Film depictions of emotionally abusive coach–athlete interactions
Gretchen Kerr, Ashley Stirling and Ahad Bandealy
Sports Coaching Review, volume 5, issue 1 (May 2016) pp. 87–101

Chapter 8
Too hot to handle? A social semiotic analysis of touching in "Bend it like Beckham"
Dean Garratt and Heather Piper
Sports Coaching Review, volume 5, issue 1 (May 2016) pp. 102–115

Chapter 9
'We're In This Together': neoliberalism and the disruption of the coach/athlete hierarchy in CrossFit
Leslie Heywood
Sports Coaching Review, volume 5, issue 1 (May 2016) pp. 116–129

For any permission-related enquiries please visit:
http://www.tandfonline.com/page/help/permissions

Notes on Contributors

Ahad Bandealy is a PhD Candidate at the Faculty of Kinesiology and Physical Education, University of Toronto, Toronto, Canada.

Katharina Bonzel is a Visiting Fellow in Screen Studies at the Australian National University, Australia, and is currently writing a book about the representation of national identity in sports films.

Nicholas Chare is Associate Professor of Modern Art in the Department of History of Art and Film Studies at the Université de Montréal, Canada. He is the author of *Sportswomen in Cinema: Film and the Frailty Myth* (2015).

Seán Crosson is Lecturer Above the Bar at the Huston School of Film and Digital Media, National University of Ireland, Galway, Republic of Ireland.

Dean Garratt is Professor of Education at the Faculty of Education and Children's Service, University of Chester, Manchester, UK.

Leslie Heywood is Professor of English and Creative Writing in the Department of English at Binghamton University – State University of New York (SUNY), Binghamton, NY, USA.

Sue Jolly is a Lecturer in the Carnegie School of Sport, Leeds Beckett University, Leeds, UK.

Gretchen Kerr is Professor in the Faculty of Kinesiology and Physical Education, University of Toronto, Toronto, Canada.

John Lyle is Professor of Sports Coaching in the Carnegie School of Sport, Leeds Beckett University, Leeds, UK.

Bryan Mead is a PhD candidate at Northern Illinois University, Dekalb, IL, USA.

Jason Mead is a teacher and basketball coach at Dixon High School, Dixon, IL, USA.

Heather Piper is Professor at the Education and Social Research Institute, Manchester Metropolitan University, Manchester, UK.

Ashley Stirling is Assistant Professor in the Faculty of Kinesiology and Physical Education, University of Toronto, Toronto, Canada.

Introduction

Sports coaching on film

Katharina Bonzel[a] and Nicholas Chare[b]

[a]College of Arts and Social Sciences, Australian National University, Canberra, Australia; [b]Department of History of Art and Film Studies, Université de Montréal, Montréal, Canada

> Oh man, if in real life I was as cool and suave as Coach Taylor and had all the answers, things would be easier. (Coach Taylor (Kyle Chandler) in the series *Friday Night Lights*)

Every inch the coach

This special issue, "Sports Coaching on Film", sets out to analyse representations of sports coaches in film and to indicate some of the ways in which the study of film depictions of coaches might be informative for actual sports coaching. The project was inspired, in significant part, by Emma Poulton's and Matthew Roderick's ground-breaking special edition of *Sport in Society*, "Sports in Films". In their Introduction to the special issue, Poulton and Roderick draw attention to how "constructions and representations of sport and athletes have been marginalised in terms of serious analysis within the long-standing academic study of films and documentaries" (2008, p. 107). There were notable exceptions to this state of neglect, scholars who had already brought the study of sports films to the fore included Aaron Baker, particularly through his book *Contesting Identities*, and Deborah Tudor who had authored *Hollywood's Vision of Team Sports* (Baker, 2003; Tudor, 1997).

The state of affairs described by Poulton and Roderick has subsequently changed with a number of important monographs and edited collections published in the past five years (e.g. Babington, 2014; Chare, 2015; Crosson, 2013; Ingle & Sutera, 2013; Lieberman, 2015). These studies foreground the importance of the study of sports films for increasing our understanding of class, ethnicity, gender, race and sexuality as they are articulated in specific cultural, social, and historical contexts. Some of these recent investigations briefly explore the significance of the figure of the sports coach. Lieberman, for instance, devotes a chapter of her book *Sports Heroines on Film* to portrayals of female coaches (pp. 126–150). There is, however, still no in-depth study focussed specifically on portrayals of coaches and coaching in sports films. This is a considerable omission given coaching forms a particularly influential dimension of athlete development. Our special

1

issue contributes to the ongoing process of bringing the coach from the sidelines of sports film scholarship to centre-field.

In *The Sports Film*, Bruce Babington (2014) suggests that the coach "is arguably the recent sports film's defining figure" (p. 102). For Babington this perceived rise to prominence reflects "modern sport's ever increasing rationalisation" and the growing reliance on coaches rather than players for decision-making with the added pressures and responsibilities that brings for the coach (p. 102). On film, the coach can come to embody "the tensions and contradictions of modern sport generally" (Babington, 2014, p. 104). The coach in sports films therefore reflects changing cultural and social conceptions of sport which in turn have been shaped by broader socio-cultural transformations. Film, however, like any art form is far from mechanistic in its reflection of dominant beliefs and values and manifests a degree of independence from them.[1] As will become clear from many of the essays in this issue, film occasionally provides visions of coaching that are at odds with prevailing approaches and accepted behaviours in real life. The coach in film is often seen as if through a glass darkly rather than clearly mirroring contemporary social mores and actual coaching practices. John Lyle (2002) suggests that claims to artistry have enabled coaches to "weave an aura of mystique about coaching" and to create "a protective occupational shell" (p. 29). This mystique may be reinforced and perpetuated through film depictions of coaching.

Coaches in film are also often understood in polarising ways, seen either to exemplify good or bad practices. Scott Crawford (1991), for instance, has analysed the figure of the "bad" coach in sports films. Crawford considers how popular cultural stereotypes of coaching are replicated in films and argues that there is inadequate character development. In this context, E.M. Forster's idea of "flat" and "round" characters in novels is enlightening (1974).[2] For Forster, flat characters are constructed around a single idea or trait. Round characters, by contrast, develop, change. For Crawford, coaches in sports films are never fleshed out. They remain stuck at the level of caricature for the entire narrative, never progressing to having character proper. Films too often sharply contrast good and bad rather than acknowledging that "elite coaches are complex chameleon personalities" (Crawford, 1992, p. 57). Similar findings have been made in relation to cinematic portrayals of physical education teachers who are consistently framed as butches, bullies or buffoons (McCullick et al., 2003).

Crawford's observation about film representations of coaches arguably has merit for the majority of films produced up until he conducted his 1992 study. This issue, however, demonstrates that simply dividing portrayals of sports coaches into the good (nice, encouraging, and empathetic) and the bad (abusive, aggressive, and dictatorial) is reductive. There has been an enduring Hollywood tendency to excise moral ambiguity from mainstream cinema, a tendency given its strongest expression not in the context of sports films but psychological thrillers. *Insomnia* the 2002 remake of the 1997 Norwegian film of the same name replaces all the subtlety and opacity of the original with a straightforward tale of choosing between right or wrong. This special issue shows, however, that recent sports films complicate either/or understandings of the sports coach, providing representations that are more nuanced and depicting behaviours that are difficult to gauge and do not invite clear-cut judgements.

Zygmunt Bauman (1991) suggests that ambivalence produces "acute discomfort" (p. 1). We do not like things that resist easy categorisation. This may explain why there has been a certain reticence in some areas of the Social Sciences to embrace film as an object of study. Film is a complex audio-visual medium that can be remarkably resistant to efforts to systematically analyse and classify, to categorise and quantify, to treat as data. We are therefore particularly grateful to those of our contributors from backgrounds that might be labelled as social scientific who have embraced our topic. A major aim of the issue from the outset was to foster dialogue across the Humanities and Social Sciences in relation to sports coaching on film. There are often distinct approaches and methodological differences between our contributors, but the essays taken as a whole include enriching and inspiring moments of crossover, most notably a shared commitment to social justice, to combatting expressions of violence and to identifying instances of oppression as they manifest in films featuring sports coaches.

In the context of social justice, it is important to remember that film as a medium is not passive. Film possesses agency, potentially intervening in and changing understandings, influencing actions. This influence can sometimes be direct and obvious. In her autobiography, for example, Jessica Ennis (2012) refers to the way her coach Toni Minichiello's conduct is inspired by cinema: "He loves the film *Any Given Sunday* and is prone to making the Al Pacino speech near the end. "You'll find out life is just a game of inches," Chell will growl as Pacino" (p. 60). Minichiello's tongue-in-cheek mimicking of the character Tony D'Amato's motivational speech-making in Oliver Stone's American football film *Any Given Sunday* raises a serious issue about the effects of fictional portrayals of coaching on real coach–athlete interactions. Pacino's character D'Amato in *Any Given Sunday* is based, in part, on Vince Lombardi, who was coach of the American football team the Green Bay Packers in the 1960s. The film is therefore influenced by sports coaching history and, in turn, influences, thus demonstrating the real-life power of sports films. In a pioneering early analysis of depictions of coaches in American football films, Douglas Noverr (1990) drew attention to how the characters of onscreen coaches are inspired by actual figures.

D'Amato also embodies the ambiguity we referred to earlier as characteristic of recent representations of coaches in sports films. He is shown in consistently contradictory terms. At once put upon and imposing, D'Amato manifests an aggressive tenderness to his charges, displays an exuberant atrabiliousness in everyday life, is old-fashioned in his approach to coaching yet this anachronistic outlook is ultimately framed as forward-thinking, bringing footballing success. Babington has interpreted him as a "split figure" who incarnates "the clashing values of pragmatism and idealism, instrumentalism and loyalty in contemporary sport" (103). *Any Given Sunday* is designed to inflame conscience as, through the divided and divisive figure of D'Amato, it explores the nefarious influence of corporate America on gridiron. The theme of corporatism, the presence of greed (here for success), positions *Any Given Sunday* as the sporting equivalent to *Wall Street* in Stone's corpus. Babington suggests the film engages with "changing actual world realities" (108). By highlighting these realities, Stone invites his audience to question their effects and query their continuing existence, taking responsibility for a situation they are embedded within. He makes use of the audio-visual as a potential catalyst for change, a possible means of acting upon the world.

More often, however, films are conservative, influencing unknowingly and reproducing the status quo unreflectively. In an important precursor to some of the analyses that follow, David Kahan's and Mensah Kutame's essay 'Observing and Analyzing a Fictional Coach's Behaviors: Implications for Coaching Education' examines how films shape beliefs about what comprises coaching practice. They suggest popular cultural media such as films provide under-examined templates for how coaches should behave. A real-life coach's behaviour is frequently shaped by their own personal historical experiences of being coached and by media images including film. Kahan and Kutame suggest that the perceptions of reality purveyed by film makers "subtly becomes our perceptions of what is real" (1997, p. 21). For this reason, it is as important to study fictional coaches as real ones.

The Lombardi inspired D'Amato of *Any Given Sunday*, with its circular relationship of art imitating life imitating art that the example of Ennis's coach demonstrates, suggests that this distinction between fiction and reality is itself questionable. In a recent essay, "That Spectacular Supplement", Paul Bowman has argued that the seemingly opposed realms of reality and representation are imbricated (2016). Bowman views distinctions between the domains of the filmic and daily life as a needless metaphysical convention. In reality, these seemingly opposed realms supplement each other. Bowman is writing in the context of martial arts films but his observations, influenced by deconstruction, are also relevant for films featuring sports coaches. In their essay "The traditional, the ideal and the unexplored", Sue Jolly and John Lyle make a similar point, suggesting in the context of *Twenty Four Seven* that the film is as much ethnographic documentary as social realist fiction. They explain that some sports documentaries similarly cross "the boundaries between fact and fiction". The capacity of film, be it documentary or fiction, to potentially impact lived behaviour is a common theme in many of the essays in this issue.

Getting in on the act

Kahan and Kutame, who focus on the ice hockey film *D2: The Mighty Ducks* for their analysis, regard coaching films as potential pedagogical tools and suggest that documentary films, in particular, might one day be made use of in training prospective coaches (32). In a sense, the two researchers regard sports films as in themselves coaching, fostering particular behaviours, fulfilling certain objectives. The idea of being coached by film is implicit in interpretation of film as a tool of ideology, as an embodiment of hegemonic values. Such a conception is at work, for example, in Seán Crosson's essay, "Configuring Irishness through Coaching Films", which provides a subtle and refined examination of *Peil* (about Gaelic football) and *Christy Ring* (about hurling) as films that do not solely provide sporting instruction for their audiences but also operate to instil particular understandings of Irishness in them. This understanding is engendered not solely through depicting Indigenous Irish sports but also through the ways in which these sports are framed. Crosson refers to the films 'coaching' viewers about Irish identity, working to fashion citizens attuned to the language, politics and religion of Éire. This coaching manifests through choice of shots, editing and the soundtrack.

In "'I love you guys': *Hoosiers* as a model for transformational and limited transactional coaching", Bryan Mead and Jason Mead consider how films featuring coaches might consciously be deployed as educational aids. For Mead and Mead, *Hoosiers* embodies many of the ideas about leadership advanced by James Kouzes and Barry Posner in their classic text, *The Leadership Challenge* (1987). This lends the film potential pedagogical value. The central character Coach Norman Dale's management skills, which are seen to epitomise the five practices of exemplary leadership, provides viewers with leadership lessons. Through a sophisticated analysis of cinematography and shot selection in *Hoosiers*, Mead and Mead demonstrate that the effectiveness of these lessons is reinforced by way of camerawork and editing. These dimensions of the film can be seen to "coach" about leadership effectiveness.

Hoosiers is loosely based on the legendary success of the 1954 Milan High School basketball team. Coached by Marvin Wood, the team defeated the significantly bigger school Muncie Central to become Indiana State Champions. Unlike the team in the film, Milan High School's win was not unexpected. *Hoosiers*, a regular in "best sports films" lists, such as the American Film Institute's *AFI's 10 Top 10* (Sports Films), has had impact beyond the confines of basketball.[3] The politician Ted Cruz, seeking to woo the voters of Indiana in the run up to a Republican primary in 2016, recreated a scene from the film as part of a speech he gave in a gym where scenes from *Hoosiers* were filmed. Cruz performed the role of Norman Dale (originally played by Gene Hackman) for his audience, recreating a famous sequence where the coach measures the height of the basket before the crucial State Championship game to seek to calm the nerves of his players: "Ten feet. I think you'll find that's the exact same measurements as our gym back in Hickory". After choreographing the taking of similar measurements, Cruz sought to channel the spirit of Dale, proclaiming "You know, the amazing thing about that basketball ring here in Indiana, it's the same height as it is in New York City and every other place in this country. And there is nothing that Hoosiers cannot do".

Here Cruz uses the demonym Hoosiers to refer to natives of Indiana. It is in the power of the people of Indiana to vote for him and slow the momentum of his main rival for the presidential nomination, the real estate mogul Donald Trump. He uses language that casts him as the underdog, with his reference to New York made in the aftermath of Trump's considerable success in a primary there. Effectively he is calling on the people to become his Norman Dale, leading him to an unlikely victory. Through rhetorical sleight, he is positioning himself as both coach and athlete. The people of Indiana are simultaneously his coach and cast as his team, underdogs with him as their underdog leader, working together they can become champions. He both patronises the people of Indiana (who are figured as "not winners") and rouses them, validating his rallying cry by reference to a state-loved film. Cruz also, unconsciously, affirms the power of cinema: "there is nothing that *Hoosiers* cannot do". He exhibits a belief that through re-staging the film something of the coach's successful leadership will rub off on him and, perhaps, some of his heroic masculinity. In their thought-provoking reading of the film, Laura Hills and Eileen Kennedy (2013) argue that Dale would make a poor youth coach because of his disciplinarian approach but he successfully embodies Hollywood masculinity, which is to say hegemonic masculinity.

Cruz is here endeavouring not solely to borrow from Dale's metaphorical play-book and emulate his "hardman" image; he is also striving to exploit emotions bound up with the film and Indiana's more general love of basketball. Trump likewise made the most of the high esteem in which basketball is held in the state by touting the endorsement of Bobby Knight, the "ornery" Indiana University basketball coach. Cruz though turned to a fictional figure from mainstream narra-tive cinema. In his estimation, Dale seemingly trumped someone such as Knight. The political manoeuvre therefore reveals something of the perceived power of the sports film to sway hearts and minds. Cruz, however, took his eye of the ball, making the cardinal error or referring to the hoop as a ring, betraying how poorly versed he actually was in language of basketball, how foreign it is to him. As a "basketball fan", he revealed himself to be a bad actor, second-rate. Cruz's efforts to incarnate the celebrated basketball coach proved superficial.

Superficiality, as already discussed, is a common concern about film depictions of coaches. Sue Jolly and John Lyle consider the danger of the lack of depth of character accorded to coaches in their essay "The traditional, the ideal and the unexplored" which involves thoughtful close readings of the films *Bend it Like Beckham* and *Twenty Four Seven*. Jolly and Lyle trace how coaching stereotypes feature, or are resisted, in the two films. They argue that the way coaches are portrayed is, in part, genre specific. Genres display similar narrative and stylistic elements, as such, films with shared properties are grouped together and cre-ate certain audience expectations. Those that intentionally set out to amuse, for example, fall under the genre "comedy", those that strive to scare comprise the genre of "horror". Tzvetan Todorov asserted that "the study of genres, which has as its starting point the historical evidence of the existence of genres, must have as its ultimate objective precisely the establishment of these properties" (1990, p. 17). Crosson (2013) has sought to establish the specific properties of the sports film genre in general in *Sport and Film* (pp. 60–65). Jolly and Lyle build on this important precursor, offering a more fine-grained analysis by focussing specifically on the figure of the coach and teasing out differences in the portrayal of coaches between major studio productions and independent or "indie" films in the sports film genre. The generic conventions at the level of coaching are shown to sometimes be different in independent films. Jolly and Lyle also reveal that the films provide varied depictions of the professionalisation of coaching contributing to ongoing debates about coaching as a valued profession.

Good coach/bad coach

Although the representation of coaches in many sports films resists easy definition as good or bad, displaying inconsistent behaviour, there are still numerous aspects of coaching practice shown in films that are clearly negative. Many of these practices, as Hills and Kennedy (2013) have shown in their thoughtful examination of representations of sports coaching, are bound up with ideas about heroism and hypermasculinity. Hills and Kennedy argue that "critical analysis of the heroic construction of coaches in film and the associated styles of masculinity could form part of a coach training programme serving as a catalyst for discussion or a basis of reflexivity" (2013, p. 50). They compellingly affirm that studying cinematic depictions of coaching, including negative practices, can aid with real life coaching.

In their article, "Film Depictions of Emotionally Abusive Coach-Athlete Interactions", Gretchen Kerr, Ashley Stirling and Ahad Bandealy examine instances of abusive interaction between coaches and athletes. The figure of the emotionally abusive coach is an enduring commonplace in cinematic representations. Kerr, Stirling and Bandealy suggest that further research is needed to ascertain whether such negative depictions function cumulatively to normalise emotionally abusive coaching practices. Stirling and Kerr have already drawn attention to how athletes are often accepting of abusive behaviours due to media influence (Stirling & Kerr, 2014). Cinema potentially plays a contributing role in the formation of this state of acceptation. It may therefore also possibly have a crucial future role to play in contesting such a state either through critically reflexive analyses of the kind championed by Hills and Kennedy or through differing representational practices adopted by film makers in relation to their portrayals of coaching. There are already exceptional films such as *Varsity Blues* which condemn "bad coaching" even as they simultaneously represent it, films which might one day become the norm.

In his article "Sound Coaching", Nicholas Chare also traces examples of abusive interactions as they manifest in the sub-genre of the American football film. Chare focusses specifically on sounds in relation to coaching, considering how dialogue, film score and sound effects, in combination with the film image, contribute to the construction of specific representations of the football coach. While these representations echo many of the lived realities of football coaching including the need to privilege emotional input at specific moments (such as during the delivery of a motivational speech), they also reinforce the pervasive sexism that still characterises gridiron. Sexism in sport is, of course, not limited to American football and neither is its depiction in sports films, something Bonzel (2013) has effectively shown in her analysis of the female athlete-coach Dottie in the baseball film *A League of Their Own*. Dottie, despite a clear understanding of the game and an impressive rapport with the team she is instructing, is replaced by a man.

American football, however, often forms an expression of hypermasculinity that is bound up with violence (Dundes, 1978) and in films featuring gridiron, the violent dynamic of the sport is frequently gendered with coaches associating femininity with delicacy and passivity and constructing it in negative terms. Weaving together analyses of both dialogue and visual elements, Chare examines ways sexism is sometimes linked to animal metaphors by football coaches in films. The long tradition of linking woman and the non-human animal in Western culture (Creed & Hoorn, 2016, pp. 90–1) is given forceful expression in the onscreen language of football coaching. Chare concludes by suggesting that both the sexism and the zoomorphism manifested by football coaches on film is bound up with their efforts to foster emotional responses in their players and, by extension, with the efforts of film makers to make their audiences feel something.

Gendered representations of coaches come into even sharper focus in Katharina Bonzel's contribution to this special issue "Mind the Gap: Female Coaches in Hollywood Sports Films". According to the movie database IMDB, of the 122 Hollywood sports films that focus on coaching produced since 1985, only three feature female coaches.[4] Focusing specifically on female coaches of men's teams, Bonzel uses close visual analysis to demonstrate that representations of female coaches are not only rare but also problematic in their stereotypical depiction of femininity in general and of women within the sporting arena in particular. Despite some of the films endeavouring to legitimize the female coach, their insistence on an essential difference between the sexes—an insistence articulated both through the narrative and by way of filmic techniques such as cinematography—means that they ultimately fail in their proposed "feminist" agenda.

In their inspiring close reading of *Bend it Like Beckham*, "Too hot to handle?", Dean Garratt and Heather Piper provide an incisive social semiotic analysis of instances of physical contact between coach and athlete as they are portrayed in the film that is impressively coupled with a consideration of the Foucauldian themes of discourse, power/knowledge and governmentality. There have been a number of consideration of visual depictions of touch in coaching recently (e.g. Chare, 2013; Jones, Bailey & Santos, 2013). Garratt and Piper, however, provide the first sustained analysis of a single case study, ably demonstrating how a close analysis of the film is enlightening in relation to the cultural politics of touch in coaching situations. At times, fiction films such as *Bend it Like Beckham* provide an alternative outlook to tactile encounters between coaches and athletes, one that is at odds with contemporary risk-averse attitudes. Touching encounters between coach and athlete in sports films are not always represented negatively. Garratt and Piper suggest, in fact, that films such as *Bend it Like Beckham* offer a reminder "of a world which we have lost but that, with some clearer thinking and good sense, we may choose to find again".

Time watching

Coaches and athletes frequently have a particularly complex relationship to time. Bruno Rigauer has examined how the use of time by athletes is meticulously controlled and regimented as part of their goal-oriented existence. Rigauer (1981) asserts that "the top-level athlete cannot train according to his [*sic*] own time plan" (p. 43). An athlete's time is closely managed by their coach. Their performance is also often assessed in temporal terms. The stopwatch is a frequent prop in film representations of coaches ranging from coach Sam Mussabini in *Chariots of Fire* finding another split second for his charge Harold Abrahams to win the gold medal in the 100m sprint, to the players gifting coach Molly McGrath a stopwatch in *Wildcats*. While the stopwatch in *Chariots* is a symbol of efficiency and mastery over time, in *Wildcats* it represents the players' acceptance of their female coach.

Rowe (2008) has considered the sometimes complex relationships sports films establish towards time. Rowe reads sports films as simultaneously bound to chronological time and able to escape its sequenced constraints. He suggests the documentary *Zidane, Un portrait du 21e siècle*, for instance, embodies a proliferation of temporalities, "from the progressive to the recursive" (Rowe, 2008, p. 156). *Zidane* displays some of the ways in which sports films possess a creativity lacking from live sports broadcasts; a creativity made particularly manifest through the multiple temporalities that the documentary is able to engender. Rowe's time-based analysis foregrounds the distance and difference between documentary sports films and fiction films and other forms of sports representation.

The majority of the contributors to this special issue chose to engage with fiction films. In "We're In This Together!" Leslie Heywood, however, provides a sophisticated analysis of temporality in the context of CrossFit coaching that centres upon analyses of two documentaries and a commercial. Heywood is a leading theorist of the CrossFit phenomenon who has previously examined ways in which CrossFit employs affective immersion to foster bonding between groups who participate in the programme (Heywood, 2015). In her current article, Heywood explores how different modalities of time manifest in CrossFit, namely "clock time" and "network time". CrossFit's temporal characteristics cannot be dissociated from the neoliberal values that are embodied in the fitness programme. Through a subtle and incisive analysis of the CrossFit documentaries *Every Second Counts* and *The Test of Fitness* and the CrossFit "Thank You Coach" commercial, Heywood demonstrates that these values impact upon the relation between athlete and coach, blurring the boundaries between the two. These differing representations cumulatively reinforce the decentralised quality of physical training in CrossFit.

Heywood reads the "Thank You Coach" commercial as reflective of the values and self-envisioning of many CrossFit coaches. The kinds of coaching visible in the commercial are far removed from the stereotypical aggressive authoritarian coaching style depicted in mainstream narrative sports films.

The "Thank You Coach" commercial that Heywood discusses is approximately a minute long yet it is clear from her beautiful, in-depth reading of the advertisement that she has studied it repeatedly. Mulvey (2006) reflects on how digital technology has permitted the "lack of smoothness that has always been an aspect of film narrative" to become amplified (p. 150). In all film media it is now easier to find and to freeze frame key shots, to repeatedly view particular scenes, than when technology such as a film projector or a VCR was required. Mulvey (2006) writes:

> In film theory and criticism, delay is the essential process behind textual analysis. The flow of a scene is halted and extracted from the wider flow of narrative development; the scene is broken down into shots and selected frames and further subjected to delay, to repetition and return. In the course of this process, hitherto unexpected meanings can be found hidden in the sequence, as it were, deferred to a point of time in the future when the critic's desire may unearth them. (p. 144)

All the articles in this issue, in their different ways, perform this kind of excavation, this archaeological labour. Film does not surrender these secrets immediately. It is a time-consuming, interminable process. Nevertheless, we believe that these directed analyses of sports coaching provide lasting insights and lay the groundwork for important future research.

Conclusion: film credits

Bringing together leading scholars in their respective fields, this collection of essays showcases the rich potential of studies of sports coaches in cinema and how these might benefit, complicate and/or even hinder actual coaching practices. We hope that our readers will agree that the diversity of approaches and contributors is a particular strength of the issue, bridging the sometimes gap between the Humanities and the Social Sciences fruitfully and to their mutual benefit. We encourage a continuation of this dialogue as there is much still to discover in the tensions between coaches and their on-screen counterparts. We want to conclude by thanking the editorial team of *Sports Coaching Review*, who enthusiastically embraced this project from the get-go, enabling us to investigate the important tensions, issues and questions that surround film depictions of sports coaching. We would also like to warmly acknowledge the many anonymous peer reviewers whose insightful comments and criticisms have proved invaluable to all of our contributors.

Notes

1. Karl Marx (1993) provides the skeleton for such an argument in *Grundrisse* using Greek art as his chosen example (pp. 110–1).

2. See Chare's (2015) chapter on boxing films in *Sportswomen in Cinema* for a lengthier discussion of how Forster's ideas about literary character can be applied in a cinematic context (pp. 41–66; pp. 57–60).
3. See http://www.afi.com/10top10/category.aspx?cat=4, accessed 29 May 2016.
4. These are the 1986 football comedy *Wildcats*, the 1996 basketball comedy *Eddie* and the 2009 drama *The Mighty Macs*. IMDB is of course only helpful in so far as one trusts its generic categorisations and keywording, and thus one further film, the 1996 drama *Sunset Park* can be added to this exclusive list of films.

Disclosure statement

No potential conflict of interest was reported by the authors.

References

Babington, B. (2014). *The sports film: Games people play*. London: Wallflower.

Baker, A. (2003). *Contesting identities: Sports in American film*. Urbana: University of Illinois Press.

Bauman, Z. (1991). *Modernity and ambivalence*. Cambridge: Polity.

Bonzel, K. (2013). *A league of their own*: The impossibility of the female sports hero. *Screening The Past, 37*, retrieved from http://www.screeningthepast.com/2013/10/a-league-of-their-own-the-impossibility-of-the-female-sports-hero/

Bowman, P. (2016). That spectacular supplement: Martial arts film as reality. In N.Chare & L.Watkins (Eds.), *Gesture and Film: Signalling New Critical Perspectives* (in press). London: Routledge.

Chare, N. (2013). Handling pressures: Analysing touch in American films about youth sport. *Sport, Education and Society, 18*, 663–677.

Chare, N. (2015). *Sportswomen in cinema: Film and the frailty myth*. London: IB Tauris.

Crawford, S. (1992). The bad coach in contemporary sporting films: An analysis of caricature, character and stereotype. *Applied Research In Coaching And Athletics Annual, 6*, 46–61.

Creed, B., & Hoorn, J. (2016). Animals, art, abjection. In R. Arya & N. Chare (Eds.), *Abject Visions: Powers of Horror in Art and Visual Culture* (pp. 90–104). Manchester: Manchester University Press.

Crosson, S. (2013). *Sport and film*. London: Routledge.

Dundes, A. (1978). Into the endzone for a touchdown: A psychoanalytic consideration of American football. *Western Folklore, 37*, 75–88.

Ennis, J. (2012). *Jessica Ennis: Unbelievable*. London: Hodder & Stoughton.

Forster, E. M. (1974). *Aspects of the novel*. London: Edward Arnold.

Heywood, L. (2015). The CrossFit sensorium: Visuality, affect and immersive sport. *Paragraph, 38*, 20–36.

Hills, L., & Kennedy, E. (2013). Ready, set, action: Representations of coaching through film. In P. Potrac, W. Gilbert, & J. Denison (Eds.), *Routledge Handbook of Sports Coaching* (pp. 40–51). London: Routledge.

Ingle, Z., & Sutera, D. M. (Eds.). (2013). *Gender and genre in sports documentaries: Critical essays*. Lanham: The Scarecrow Press.

Jones, R. L., Bailey, J., & Santos, S. (2013). Coaching, caring and the politics of touch: A visual exploration. *Sport, Education and Society, 18*, 648–662.

Kahan, D., & Kutame, M. (1997). Observing and analyzing a fictional coach's behaviors: Implications for coaching education. *Applied Research In Coaching And Athletics Annual, 12*, 19–34.

Kouzes, J., & Posner, B. (1987). *The leadership challenge*. New York, NY: Wiley.

Lieberman, V. (2015). *Sports heroines on film: A critical study of cinematic women athletes, coaches and owners*. Jefferson, NC: McFarland.

Lyle, J. (2002). *Sports coaching concepts: A framework for coaches' behaviour*. Abingdon: Routledge.

Marx, K. (1993[1939]). *Grundrisse: Foundations of the critique of political economy (rough draft)*. London: Penguin.

McCullick, B., Belcher, D., Hardin, B., & Hardin, M. (2003). Butches, bullies, and buffoons: Images of physical education teachers in the movies. *Sport, Education And Society, 8*, 3–16.

Mulvey, L. (2006). *Death 24x a second*. London: Reaktion.

Noverr, D. (1990). The coach and the athlete in football sports films. In P. Loukides & L. K. Fuller (Eds.), *Beyond the Stars: Studies in American Popular Film* (pp. 120–130). Bowling Green: Bowling Green State University Press.

Poulton, E. & Roderick, M. (2008). *Sport in Films*. London: Routledge.

Rigauer, B. (1981). *Sport and work*. New York, NY: Columbia University Press.

Rowe, D. (2008). Time and timelessness in sport film. *Sport in Society, 11*, 146–158.

Stirling, A. E., & Kerr, G. (2014). Initiating and sustaining emotional abuse in the coach–athlete relationship: An ecological transactional model of vulnerability. *Journal of Aggression, Maltreatment & Trauma, 23*, 116–125.

Todorov, T. (1990). *Genres in discourse*. Cambridge: Cambridge University Press.

Tudor, D. (1997). *Hollywood's vision of team sports: Heroes, race, and gender*. New York, NY: Garland.

Filmography

Marshall, P., & Abbott, E. (1992). *A league of their own*. United States: Columbia Pictures.

Stone, O., & Donner, R. (1999). *Any Given Sunday*. United States: Warner Bros. Pictures.

Chadha, G. (2002). *Bend it like Beckham*. United Kingdom: Rank Film Distribution.

Hudson, H, & Puttnam, D. (1981) *Chariots of fire*. United Kingdom: Warner Bros. Pictures/20th Century Fox.

Marcus, L., Móráin, Ó., & D., (1964). *Christy Ring*. Ireland: Gael Linn.

Weisman, S., & Avnet, J. (1994). *D2: The mighty ducks*. United States: Buena Vista Pictures.

Rash, S., & Permut, D. (1996). *Eddie*. United States: Buena Vista Pictures/PolyGram Filmed Entertainment.

Matossian, S., & Peterson, C. (2009). *Every second counts*. USA: CrossFit Pictures.

Anspaugh, D., & De Haven, C. (1986). *Hoosiers*. United States: Orion Pictures.

Skjoldbjærg, E., & Backstrom, T. (1997). *Insomnia*. Norway: Norsk Filmdistribusjon/First Run Features.

Nolan, C., & Witt, P. J. (2002). *Insomnia*. United States: Warner Bros. Pictures.

Chambers, T. (2009). *The mighty macs*. United States: Freestyle Releasing.

Cannon, H., & Glancy, J. (2014). *The test of fitness*. USA: CrossFit.

Marcus, L., Móráin, Ó., & D., (1962). *Peil*. Ireland: Gael Linn.

REPRESENTATIONS OF SPORT COACHES IN FILM

Gomer, S., & DeVito, D. (1996). *Sunset park*. United States: TriStar Pictures.

West, I., & Meadows, S. (1998). *Twenty four seven*. United Kingdom: Pathé.

Robbins, B. (1999). *Varsity blues*. United States: Paramount Pictures.

Stone, O., & Pressman, E.R. (1987) *Wall street*. United States: 20th Century Fox.

Ritchie, M., & Sylbert, A. (1986). *Wildcats*. United States: Warner Bros. Pictures.

Gordon, D., & Sighvatsson, S. (2006). *Zidane: Un portrait du 21e siècle*. France: Ana Lena Films.

Configuring Irishness through coaching films: *Peil* (1962) and *Christy Ring* (1964)

Seán Crosson

Huston School of Film and Digital Media, National University of Ireland, Galway, Republic of Ireland

ABSTRACT

The sports coaching film has a long history, dating from at least 1932 with the production of Paulette McDonagh's *How I Play Cricket* which featured the legendary Don Bradman. However, coaching films dedicated to indigenous Irish sport, or Gaelic games, are a more recent development, emerging in the late 1950s. This article considers two such films – *Peil* (Louis Marcus, 1962) and *Christy Ring* (Louis Marcus, 1964) – dedicated to Gaelic football and hurling, respectively, and produced by the Irish-language cultural organisation Gael Linn. The principal concern in undertaking this examination is to identify the process by which these films configure Irishness, not just through the depictions of the indigenous sports featured but also through the manner in which these depictions are framed. In "configuring Irishness", the article examines in particular how these films articulate Irish identity and its constituent properties, particularly in terms of language, geography, politics and religion, thereby "coaching" viewers in Irishness itself, its features, and Ireland's political and moral leaders.

The sports coaching film has a long history, dating from at least 1932 with the production of Paulette McDonagh's *How I Play Cricket* which featured the legendary Don Bradman. However, coaching films dedicated to indigenous Irish sport, or Gaelic games, are a more recent development, emerging in the late 1950s. This article considers two such films – *Peil* (Dir. Louis Marcus, Ireland, 1962) and *Christy Ring* (Dir. Louis Marcus, Ireland, 1964) – dedicated to Gaelic football and hurling respectively and produced by the Irish-language cultural organisation Gael Linn. The principal concern in undertaking this examination is to identify the process by which these films configure Irishness, not just through the depictions of the indigenous sports themselves but also through the manner in which these depictions are framed. In "configuring Irishness", I am referring specifically "to the manner through which these films articulate Irish identity and its constituent properties, particularly in terms of language, geography, politics and religion. The relationship of sport with national culture and identity is a complex yet crucial one in understanding the popularity and passions that sport evokes internationally. A key force in the promotion of nationalism is culture; as Ernest Gellner notes "culture is now the necessary shared medium" (Gellner, 1983, pp. 37–38) and sport is one of the most popular of such cultural activities, contributing considerably to citizens' identification with particular nations. Moreover, in emphasising the banality of nationalism as a "natural" and often unnoticed part of everyday life, Michael Billig has argued that modern sport has a social and political signifi- cance that "extend[s] through the media beyond the player and the spectator" (Billig, 1995, p. 120) by providing luminous moments of national engagement and national heroes whom citizens can emulate and adore. As Billig's remarks suggest, the mass media (including the cinema) has had a crucial role to play in the popularisation of sport and, indeed, in asserting its political significance. Film's potential as a powerful vehicle for the articulation and affirmation of the nation has been recognised in critical studies (Higson, 1995; Hjort & Mackenzie, 2000). Susan Hayward in her study of French cinema identified how film may function

> as a cultural articulation of a nation …[it] textualises the nation and subsequently constructs a series of relations around the concepts, first, of state and citizen, then of state, citizen and other … a "national" cinema … is ineluctably "reduced" to a series of enunciations that reverberate around two fundamental concepts: identity and differ- ence (2005, p. x).

This article will examine, through close readings of *Peil* and *Christy Ring*, pre- cisely this process whereby these coaching films "textualise" the Irish nation.

Coaching Irishness through film

As Hills and Kennedy have noted, representations of coaching in films do more than provide us with an opportunity to examine the various masculinities (the predominant focus) constructed in particular sporting contexts; they also offer a means "to understand the ways that, as an audience, we are being asked to make sense of the relationships between them" (Hills & Kennedy, 2013, p. 41). For the purposes of this study, I wish to consider the manner through which both *Peil* and *Christy Ring* configure Irishness and the role they may play not only in coaching young people in how to play Gaelic games but also "coaching" viewers – and particularly impressionable children and young adults who would have been a principal target audience for these films – on the nature of Irishness itself as an identity construct, including in terms of language, geography, politics and reli- gion. As noted above by Hills and Kennedy, I similarly wish to "understand the ways that, as an audience, we are being asked to make sense of" Irish identity as constructed in these films. Such representations, of course, cannot be separated from larger social processes and indeed are part of a process which (in Hayward's terms) "textualises the nation" (Hayward, 2005, p. x). Film has a crucial role in this process, in the manner through which cultural identity is framed and depicted for popular consumption. Coaching films in particular provide fascinating texts to examine in this respect, as much for the manner in which they locate and contextualise a particular sport within a given society as for the instructions they may provide for the sport itself. With respect to *Peil* and *Christy Ring*, this is particularly evident in the manner through which these films reflect the position of the Catholic Church as the moral authority (with considerable effective political influence) in Irish society in the mid-twentieth century.

Post-Independent Ireland, the media and sport

A further emphasis identified by Susan Hayward in national cinemas, "identity and difference", was a recurring concern of the Irish political and cultural establishment from the emergence of the Irish Free State in 1922. Particularly in the decades immediately after independence, an array of organisations promoted indigenous Irish culture and institutions, and asserted the distinctiveness of Ireland from Britain politically, economically, religiously and culturally. Simultaneously, considerable efforts were made – most obviously through the Censorship of Films Act (1923) (one of the first pieces of legislation passed by the newly independent Irish Free-State) – to control the distribution and exhibition of material considered potentially counterproductive to this goal (Rockett, 2004). As this project developed apace, the growth in popularity of organised sport, particularly Gaelic games in Ireland acquired a particular importance. With the rapid rise in membership and attendances at its games across the country, the Gaelic Athletic Association (or GAA, the organisation which administers Gaelic games in Ireland) emerged as the most popular mass movement for the expression of independent Irish identity. The association's principal games, hurling and Gaelic football, established a reputation as the definitively Irish national sports as the nation building project of the Irish Free State developed (Crosson & McAnallen, 2011).

The print media and radio played a crucial role in underscoring the centrality of Gaelic games to Irish life at this time, but film would also play an important role, particularly with the establishment of the National Film Institute of Ireland (NFI) in 1945 and through the institute's films of all-Ireland finals in Gaelic football and hurling produced from 1948 until the late 1960s (Crosson, 2013). From 1959 to 1963, Gael Linn, an organisation devoted to the promotion of the Irish language and culture, included Gaelic games among the subjects covered in its weekly "Amharc Éireann" newsreel series. Indeed, sport and the cinema were in some respects complementary forces in the rise and development of Irish nationalism in this period. As Mike Cronin has argued in *Sport and Irish Nationalism*, sport, by virtue of being "low culture and the passion of the many", is an ideal vehicle used to understand popular Irish nationalism (Cronin, 1999, pp. 18–19); and cinema likewise appealed across all sections of society and acquired a large following particularly among the working classes (Beere, 1935–1936). Hence, throughout the early to mid-twentieth century, nationalist Ireland repeatedly used sport, and particularly in the immediate post-war era, the cinema, to encourage support for its cause.

Gael Linn, Gaelic games and film

The decision of the Irish language cultural organisation Gael Linn to film Gaelic games was inseparable from the overall concerns of the organisation. While there was undoubtedly a public interest in the sports the "Amharc Éireann" series featured, more important still for the series producers was the distinctiveness of the sports depicted and their recognition as authentic aspects of Irish culture (Pratschke, 2005). As the title of the organisation indicates – a play on Irish (Gaelic) words between "Irish pool" and "Irish with us" – Irishness was indeed a defining characteristic of Gael Linn from its inception. Above all, for Gael Linn's founders, the Irish language, its preservation and promotion was a central concern. However, the beginnings of Gael Linn were also inseparable from Gaelic games; the organisation began as a fund-raising project to support initiatives to promote the Irish language and culture, organising a weekly "pool" or sports lottery based on predicting the outcome of matches in hurling and Gaelic football on the model set by the football pools in England.[1] Within a few years of its formation, Gael Linn was sponsoring several Gaelic games competitions including a Gaelic football senior tournament,[2] while the major provincial competition for elite-level players of camogie – the female equivalent of hurling – has been the Gael Linn Cup since 1956.

Gael Linn was founded in 1952 by Dónal Ó Móráin, and under Ó Móráin's guidance, the organisation recognised that film could be an important tool in the promotion of the Irish language. Ó Móráin contacted filmmaker Colm Ó Laoghaire, whom he had known from university, in early 1956 and after some discussion they decided to produce a monthly newsreel series concerned with Irish subjects and exhibited with Irish commentary. The first monthly *éagrán* or edition appeared in June 1956 and a total of 36 episodes were produced reaching an estimated audience of approximately quarter of a million each month (O'Brien, 2004, p. 105). In 1959, the series increased to weekly multi-item editions and 160 episodes were produced before its eventual discontinuation in July 1964, due both to declining cinema attendances and the arrival of television in Ireland with the opening of the national broadcaster Telefís Éireann on New Year's Eve, 1961 (Pratschke, 2005).

Inspired by the success of their weekly newsreel, Gael Linn also began to develop longer productions, beginning with the two Gaelic games coaching films, *Peil* (1962) and *Christy Ring* (1964). These films can be viewed in common with the films produced by the NFI as part of what has been described as a second cultural revival which began in the immediate post-war era (Pratschke, 2005,

p. 36). This revival was evident with the increased engagement by the Irish public with indigenous aspects of Irish culture, including sport. Gaelic games experienced record attendances in this period, increasing dramatically to over 85,000 for All-Ireland hurling final day in the mid-1950s and over 90,000 for the All-Ireland football final by 1961 (Corry, 2005, pp. 371–412).[3] This engagement with indigenous culture occured significantly at a time of considerable challenges and ultimately great change in Irish society. While the 1950s was a decade of record unemployment and emigration, the 1960s was a period of considerable economic growth following a fundamental change in policy by the Irish government. The appointment of Seán Lemass as Taoiseach (Prime Minister) in 1959 heralded a new era of economic expansion and cultural change, inspired by the economic expansionist plans of the secretary of the Department of Finance, T.K. Whitaker. This change of focus, from the economic nationalism associated with previous premier Éamon de Valera, also accelerated the transformation of Ireland from a primarily rural society to an increasingly urban one while opening the country to new economic, political and cultural influences, including following the launch of Ireland's first indigenous television channel, Telefís Éireann (today known as RTÉ). While Lemass's policies brought economic success in the 1960s, Terence Brown has documented the "much concerned, even heated, discussion" which the rapid changes in Irish society prompted. Central to this debate was the issue of national identity, "in circumstances", as Brown continues, "where many of the traditional essentialist definitions – language, tradition, culture and distinctive ideology – were widely felt to fly in the face of social reality" (Brown, 2004, p. 255).

In summary, while Irish society was undergoing a period of considerable change, a growing engagement with traditional culture, including sport, became evident in the 1960s (Brown, 2004, pp. 262–263). "'Tradition' as Simon J. Bronner has noted, 'guides and safeguards continuity in a world of change' (Bronner, 1992, p. 1). Gael Linn's coaching films were produced and distributed, therefore, within a context in which Irish identity was a recurring concern. This context ensured that these productions would ultimately constitute much more than just coaching films for Gaelic games" enthusiasts; they were important renderings and affirmations of Irish identity.

Peil (1962), *Christy Ring* (1964) and coaching Gaelic games

The importance of coaching films such as *Peil* and *Christy Ring* was underscored by the scarcity more generally of coaching materials for Gaelic games in the early twentieth century. With the exception of former Kerry captain Dick Fitzgerald's *How to play Gaelic football* (1914) and an instructional manual by former Kildare footballer Larry Stanley (circulated only among fellow Garda (the Irish police force) members in the 1940s), limited instructional material existed prior to the 1960s (Corry, 2010, p. 3). In 1958, the legendary Kerry coach Dr. Eamonn O

Sullivan produced the influential work *The Art and Science of Gaelic football* and the following year the first film work dedicated to coaching Gaelic games, Father Moran's *Skills of Gaelic Football* (1959), was produced. *Peil* and *Christy Ring*, therefore, were produced in a context of increasing focus on the importance of instructional material for Gaelic games.

The films were produced by Gael Linn in 1962 and 1964, respectively, and each was directed by Louis Marcus. Initially Gael Linn planned to produce two coaching films on Gaelic football and hurling respectively on 16 mm that could be used as coaching aids in schools but eventually it was decided to produce the two works on 35 mm and in colour for cinema distribution, due to the popular interest in Gaelic games across Ireland (Marcus, 2008). 16 mm copies were also produced for circulation to schools and colleges across the country (Hickey, 1962, p. 17). The premières of both films were major national events attended by the political leaders of the day and given wide coverage in the national media. President Éamon de Valera attended the première of *Peil* on Saturday, 24 November 1962, at the Metropole Cinema on O'Connell Street, Dublin (Marcus, 2008). Also present were the Minster for Social Welfare, Kevin Boland TD, the leader of the Irish Senate, Thomas Ó Maoláin and the Chief of Staff of the Irish Army, Leut. General John McKeown ("Football Film"). *Christy Ring* had its première at the Savoy Cinema in Cork city on 16 October 1964 and in attendance was the then Minister for Industry & Commerce (and future Taoiseach), Jack Lynch TD, who was a former team mate of Ring on the Cork hurling team (Marcus). Also present were the Lord Mayor of Cork, A.A. Healy, as well as members of the Dáil (Irish Parliament, lower house) and Seanad (upper house), including Senators T.T. O Sullivan and S. Dooge, Fine Gael TD Sean Collins, and leading members of the Cork business community ("Premiere of 'Christy Ring' film in Cork"). These premières were also described in the media as more than just occasions for the launch of coaching films; they were events of national importance in the promotion of Irish culture. D. R. Mott (General Manager of the films' sponsors, tobacco company W.D. and H.O. Wills) congratulated Gael Linn at the premiere of *Christy Ring*, not just for producing the films but also for "the progress they are making in supporting all things Irish" ("Premiere of 'Christy Ring' film in Cork"). In the figure of legendary Cork hurler Christy Ring, around whom the hurling film is based, commentators found a figure not just exemplary as a sportsman ("the very personification of hurling" (Puirseal, 1964, p. 19)) but as an Irishman. The remarks of Padraig Puirseal in the *Irish Press* following *Christy Ring*'s première are indicative of the response in the Irish media more generally to both Ring as a person and the film itself:

> To those of us who remember the decades when 'Ringey' bestrode the whole hurling world a Colossus poised on a flashing ashen blade it is truly amazing how, through brief flashbacks to matches, to newspaper headlines, to 'still' pictures, Louis Marcus recaptures the aura not along (*sic*) of greatness but almost of invincibility that the Maestro from Cloyne carried with him onto so many fields through so many years ... To me, as to most of those present in the Cork Savoy last Friday and who had like myself,

been reared on the hurling fields, those instructional sequences were nothing short of sensational for, in them Christy Ring goes far beyond the basic skills of hurling. Here the sorcerer goes near to revealing the very sources of his own magic, the Maestro lays bare, to a remarkable extent, the secrets of his own success (Puirseal, 1964, p. 19).

Foregrounding the Irish public

A significant feature of both *Peil* and *Christy Ring* is the recurring focus on the crowds attending the Gaelic games featured in each production. Following the opening credits, *Peil* begins significantly not with a shot of a game, players or even a playing pitch, but rather with a shot of the crowd attending a Gaelic football match. Indeed, the majority of the opening scenes consist of crowd shots rather than play. While foregrounding the popularity of the sport featured, these images also indicate that what we will encounter in this film has resonance beyond the game itself; resonance for an entire culture and society. As the commentator remarks in Irish, "The crowd is gathered, the stands are full, every eye directed on the playing field". *Peil* and *Christy Ring* each foreground repeatedly the social and cultural life around Gaelic games, as much as the games themselves. In *Peil*, we are brought into the bars and the conversations of men (and only men are depicted here): we are told that the games live on in argument, memory and folklore. This is the field of memories and opinions; here the players of old take on the men of today. This contention is made and confirmed in an expository style as the narrator's words are confirmed in footage of players from previous decades on the screen, superimposed over middle-aged suit-wearing men talking in an Irish bar. These scenes include footage from All-Ireland winning teams from the past parading and playing in Croke Park, footage taken from highlights preserved by the NFI. In the focus of this section, the film places considerable stress on the reception of Gaelic games, on memory, and indeed the role that film can play in this regard, in recalling and preserving.

Christy Ring also foregrounds the social context around hurling, moving from a survey of Irish legend and history (and hurling's role in it) to its contemporary importance. The film begins with an introduction to the game of hurling, as the narrator (over shots of inter-county encounters) highlights the game's distinctiveness, reputed antiquity and its centrality to Irish history and identity. It is, we are told through Irish, "the fastest field sport in the world, a game played on the fields of Tara and in Eamhain Mhacha ... the games of the Fianna and Cúchulainn" referring to the seats of Kings of Ireland and Ulster in Medieval times, as well as legendary figures in Irish mythology. Beyond its connection with these legendary figures, the narrator also draws parallels between the history of hurling and that of the Irish people themselves under colonialism, underlining hurling's political significance as a sport banned by the Normans (who invaded Ireland in the twelfth century, conquering large parts of the country) but reflecting "the resilience of the people that almost perished before the spirit of the country revived". In this introduction and these words, hurling is presented as much more than a popular Irish pastime; it is a sport that represents the Irish people, their turbulent past and challenging present.

Christy Ring moves from an introduction to the sport, country and player to the buildup to a game featuring Ring, at the Athletic Grounds in Cork (Ring's home county) for a hurling encounter between Cork and Tipperary, "two counties" as the legendary broadcaster and commentator Michael O'Hehir remarks on the soundtrack, "famed in history, famed in song and famed in story as the greats of hurling". A strong emphasis is placed on the engagement of Irish people with hurling as an important part of their life. As with *Peil*, considerable time is given in *Christy Ring* to the rendering of the buildup to the hurling game featured, including the arrival of crowds, foregrounded repeatedly as the credit sequence roles, and at the pre-match ceremony. We watch supporters making their way, stopping occasionally for cups of tea as they travel by car, van, bus, foot, and boat (crossing the river Lee to the stadium) for the game featured.

As an important point of identification for Irish audiences watching each film, these crowd scenes engage viewers still further with sports they are already familiar with and enthusiastic regarding. However, this foregrounding of the crowd ultimately involves more than just identification with the sport itself, as very quickly becomes clear in the footage presented in *Peil*. Within the first minute of the film, we are presented not just with shots of the crowd but with a prominent shot of their moral and political leaders in Irish society at the time. While the commentary in Irish reminds us that every age and class is present, "clergy, politicians, teenagers, farmers, housewives", we are presented with a shot of the President, Taoiseach (Prime Minister), and a senior Catholic Cleric (Figure 1) in the VIP section of the Hogan stand at Croke Park. In one image, the film renders the political and moral establishment of the country and affirms the significance of what we are to encounter beyond the field of sport.

Demonstrating the skills

Once the context and social importance of both Gaelic football and hurling are established in both films, the focus moves to demonstrations of the distinctive skills of each sport. In *Peil*, the skills are presented by leading contemporary players from counties across Ireland, and significantly for a Gael Linn film, this section was available with both English and Irish narration (as well as titles in both languages), indicating that the Irish language organisation could be practical as to the need to have English available for this section to ensure people could understand the rules presented. Each individual skill is presented in scenes shot in an empty Croke Park but accompanied by footage from previous Gaelic matches to demonstrate the skill in action in an actual game.

While *Peil* features a range of Gaelic footballers from counties across the island (including several from county Down, the All-Ireland champions at the time of

Figure 1. (from right to left) President Éamon de Valera, Taoiseach Seán Lemass and a senior unidentified Catholic cleric. *Peil* (1962).

the production of the film) demonstrating the skills of the game, *Christy Ring*, as the film's title suggests, focuses principally on the life and skills of a legendary figure in the history of hurling. It is Ring who demonstrates the skills of the game (with each skill introduced with wide shots of the particular skill evident during hurling games in Croke Park) and the film is an important record in this respect of one of the finest exponents of hurling. While the narration continues in Irish, Ring's own introduction and comments on each skill are delivered in English. The titles are also provided in both English and Irish. As with the introduction to the film as a whole, this skills' demonstration is not without political resonances; it is accompanied by a marching instrumental version of the popular nationalist song "Clare's Dragoons", also featured in the opening credit sequence of *Peil*. "Clare's Dragoons" was composed by Thomas Osborne Davis (1814–1845), a poet and the principal organiser of the nationalist Young Ireland movement in the mid-19th century. The song itself is an ode to a battalion which fought during the Williamite War in Ireland (1688–1691) with the Catholic forces under King James II against the army of William III of England.

In addition to the political resonance of the accompanying music, the instructional approach adopted to the skills of each game featured remain with the viewer throughout both *Peil* and *Christy Ring*, even where skills may not be presented. Admonitions such as "if done correctly", "should be made only", "it is vital", "should be reserved", "should be kept", "never think in terms", "should be practiced" (as delivered by a player of the stature of Christy Ring in his presentation of the skills of hurling) arguably continue to inform viewers (particularly young audience members learning the skills of Gaelic games, a principal target for these films) as they encounter other aspects of Irish society and culture, including the respect and status accorded to markers of Irishness depicted in the film, as well as social and religious leaders in Irish society.

Uniting the nation

Following the demonstration of the skills, both *Peil* and *Christy Ring* return to the depiction of a match in each code. In *Peil*, the match featured is the 1960 All-Ireland football final between Kerry and Down. As with previous sequences, this coverage focuses again as much on the social occasion and those attending the game as on the game itself. This includes several minutes depicting the buildup to the game outside the stadium, including supporters arriving by foot, by car and by match day buses to the stadium with the narrator informing us in Irish that "today more than ever this is the centre of Ireland, they are here from every place, from North and South, crowds from the West and the midlands".

When we finally enter Croke Park stadium, the commentary changes to a combination of Irish and English by broadcaster Michael O'Hehir. Our arrival in Croke Park is again significantly focused initially and repeatedly on the "huge crowd" (as O'Hehir describes it) in attendance and their responses to the events unfolding. The attendance at this all-Ireland was indeed 'huge' exceeding all previous finals with almost 90,000 people present (Corry, 2005, pp. 371–412).

A considerable focus is given in both *Peil* and *Christy Ring* to the ceremony which precedes major Gaelic football and hurling encounters, including the arrival of the teams onto the pitch, the photographing of the teams by the many photographers present, and the attendance of senior figures in Irish society. In *Peil*, this sequence includes a further shot of the VIP section which again foregrounds political and moral leaders in Irish society, including President Eamon de Valera and then patron of the GAA, Archbishop of Cashel and Emly, Dr. Thomas Morris. A striking feature of this extraordinary shot is not just the prominence of red (also the colour of non-liturgical dress of Cardinals in the Catholic church) velvet furnishing but the large number of religious present in the VIP section (evident by their white collars) (Figure 2). In microcosm, this captures a crucial aspect of Irish society visually in a powerfully suggestive manner; such was the authority and influence of the Catholic Church in early 1960s Ireland that few questions would have been asked of the position accorded them at such games.

The moral authority of the Catholic church is also foregrounded in *Christy Ring*. In addition to the commentary in Irish, the review of Ring's career in the early section of the film is relayed via photographs, newspaper cuttings and short extracts from films produced by the NFI. Included among the images of Ring is a photo of him kissing the ring of a Catholic Bishop prior to the start of a game (Figure 3), a practice that continued for major Gaelic games in Croke Park until the end of the 1960s.

Figure 2. *Peil* (1962) Still of VIP section at 1960 All-Ireland football final with President Éamon de Valera to the foreground surrounded by senior religious figures including then patron of the GAA, Archbishop of Cashel and Emly, Dr. Thomas Morris (to de Valera's right).

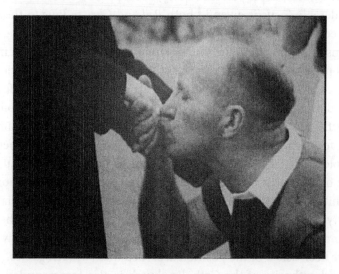

Figure 3. *Christy Ring* (1964). Still of Christy Ring kissing the ring of a Catholic bishop prior to the start of a game.

Peil's depiction of the pre-match ceremony includes the parade of the teams participating behind the Artane Boys band (a regular feature of All-Ireland final days) and the singing of the Irish national anthem, with all players standing to attention and facing the Irish national flag, captured flying over the Hogan Stand while the anthem is sung. This foregrounding of the anthem (a particularly nationalistic and militaristic piece) and Irish tricolor in *Peil* is not merely the rendering of a pre-match ceremony; it has important political connotations. This was only the second All-Ireland final in which a county from "across the border" in the disputed Northern Ireland region participated, then as now a part of the United Kingdom and subject to a different flag and anthem. Whether intentional or not, the depiction of this ceremony affirms a nationalist reading of the Irish nation (contributed to by the earlier comments by O'Hehir on the soundtrack regarding the nation encompassing people from North, South etc.) which ignores the political realities on the ground while promoting a utopian vision of a 32 county country that arguably could only be sustained (if at all) through sporting contest. While foregrounding this utopian political narrative, this depiction simultaneously reaffirms the place of the Catholic church as the moral arbiters of Irish society as it is the then patron of the GAA "the most reverend Dr. Morris" (O'Hehir's commentary) Archbishop of Cashel and Emly who gets proceedings under way by throwing the ball in among the players, a practice that was the customary beginning to All-Irelands until the late-1960s.

The footage of the game featured in *Peil* is also noticeable for its focus on the crowd and, frequently, members of the clergy attending. Many of the crowd shots at half time also feature children. Their inclusion no doubt again reflected an important intended audience of the film – children learning the skills of Gaelic football – and the hope that such shots might provide a point of further engagement for this potential audience. It is noticeable that the majority of the individuals featured in crowd shots are men and boys. While a number of women are featured, girls are noticeably absent. For a contemporary audience, the movement from shots of children, to adults, and priests, affirms the centrality and (given the elevated authority of the Catholic Church in Ireland in this period) the status of the sport featured, as well as the hierarchical structuring of Irish society in the period. Here again this audience is being coached not just in the skills of the sport featured in this film – Gaelic football – but in the structures and functioning of authority within their culture.

In *Christy Ring*, the demonstration of skills section is also followed by a return to the game that opened the documentary featuring a hurling encounter between Cork and Tipperary. Here also a considerable focus is given to the pre-match events and the crowd attending. As commentator Michael O'Hehir remarks, "whoever wins, whoever loses, thousands have come to see Christy Ring". And as with the footage in *Peil*, the playing of the national anthem is also featured prominently with players and supporters standing to respect the flag and anthem.

In *Peil*, to close both the final match footage and film as a whole, the documentary ends with the presentation of the trophy, the Sam Maguire Cup, to the captain of the winning team, Down. In this ceremony, church and state come together (in the person of Archbishop Morris and President de Valera) to affirm the role of

Figure 4. Closing Still from *Peil* (1962) featuring the presentation of the All-Ireland trophy to the Down captain by President Éamon de Valera. In the centre of the still is then patron of the GAA, Archbishop of Cashel and Emly, Dr. Thomas Morris.

Gaelic games in Irish life while simultaneously confirming the political and moral order in Irish society, as evident in Figure 4, one of the final moments in the film.

Conclusion

Film has grown in importance as an important aid in coaching since the first coaching films appeared in the early 1930s. Though coaching films dedicated to Gaelic games arrived considerably later than those focused on more international sports such as cricket and association football, both *Peil* and *Christy Ring* offer nonetheless an important record of the skills of Gaelic football and hurling respectively, as demonstrated by leading exponents of both sports in the mid-twentieth century. However, these films simultaneously function as much more than opportunities to coach Irish youth in the skills of indigenous sport; they are crucial tools in coaching these same children in Irishness itself, its features, and Ireland's political and moral leaders. If film may function, in the words of Susan Hayward, as "a cultural articulation of a nation", contributing significantly to its "textualization", then productions such as *Peil* and *Christy Ring* represent some of the most relevant and influential examples. *Peil* and *Christy Ring* present uplifting visions of Irish culture and society, foregrounding repeatedly the Irish nation, its language and culture, and social, political and religious hierarchy within a utopian configuration of a 32-county united Ireland. The role assigned to the Catholic Church within such a configuration is substantial and unquestioned. These films were arguably all the more affective as they are not didactic (with the exception of those passages instructing viewers in the skills of each sport) but rather present these features as natural, established and unquestionable aspects of Irish identity and society, thereby providing crucial affirmations of Irish society and culture at a point of considerable change and transition in its history.

Notes

1. For further on this, see Gael Linn's own website here: http://www.gael-linn.ie/default. aspx?treeid=256
2. For a notice for a game between counties Leitrim and Roscommon in the Gael Linn senior football tournament see the *Leitrim Observer*, Saturday, September 18, 1965, p. 8.
3. The All-Ireland finals (hosted normally at Croke Park Stadium in Dublin) are the final games of the principal competitions, the All-Ireland championships, held for both codes annually.

Disclosure statement

No potential conflict of interest was reported by the authors.

References

Billig, M. (1995). *Banal nationalism*. London: Sage.

Beere, T. J. (1935–1936). Cinema statistics in Saorstat Eireann. *Journal of the Statistical and Social Enquiry Society of Ireland, 156*, 83–106.

Bronner, S. J. (1992). *Creativity and tradition in folklore: New directions*. Utah: Utah State University.

Brown, T. (2004). *Ireland: A social and cultural history 1922–2002*. London: Harper Perennial.

Corry, E. (2005). *The GAA book of lists*. Dublin: Hodder Headline.

Corry, E. (2010). *The history of Gaelic Football*. Dublin: Gill & Macmillan.

Cronin, M. (1999). *Sport and Nationalism in Ireland: Gaelic games, Soccer and Irish. Identity since 1884*. Dublin: Four Courts Press.

Crosson, S. (2013). "Ar son an náisiúin": The national film institute of Ireland's all-Ireland films. *Éire-Ireland*, Special Issue on Irish Sport. *48*, 193–212.

Crosson, S., & McAnallen, D. (2011). 'Croke Park goes Plumb Crazy': Pathé Newsreels and Gaelic Games. *Media History, 17*, 161–176.

Gellner, E. (1983). *Nations and nationalism*. Oxford: Blackwell.

Hayward, S. (2005) *French national cinema*. London: Routledge.

Hickey, J. D. (1962, November 27). Football film is great success. *Irish Independent*, p. 17.

Higson, A. (1995). *Waving the flag: Constructing a national cinema in Britain.* Oxford: Clarendon Press.

Hills, L., & Kennedy, E. (2013). Ready, set, action: Representations of coaching through film. In P. Potrac, W. Gilbert, & J. Denison (Eds.), *Routledge handbook of sports coaching* (pp. 40–51). London: Routledge.

Hjort, M., & Mackenzie, S. (Eds.). (2000). *Cinema and Nation.* London: Routledge.

Marcus, L. (2008). *The making of Christy Ring and Peil. DVD notes to Christy Ring/Peil.* Dublin: Gael Linn.

O'Brien, H. (2004). *The real Ireland: The evolution of Ireland in documentary film.* Manchester, NH: Manchester University Press.

Peil. (1962). *Dir. Louis Marcus.* Dublin: Gael linn.

Pratschke, B. M. (2005). A look at Irish-Ireland: Gael Linn's Amharc Eireann Films, 1956–64. *New Hibernia Review, 9,* 17–38.

Puirseal, P. (1964, October 23). Hurling Sorcery on the screen. *Irish Press,* p. 19.

Ring, C. (1964). *Dir Louis Marcus.* Dublin: Gael linn.

Rockett, K. (2004). *Irish film censorship: A cultural journey from silent cinema to internet pornography.* Dublin: Four Courts Press.

"I love you guys": *Hoosiers* as a model for transformational and limited transactional coaching

Bryan Mead[a] and Jason Mead[b]

[a]English Department, Northern Illinois University, Dekalb, IL, USA; [b]Dixon High School, Dixon, IL, USA

ABSTRACT

This interpretive paper explores the relationship between real-world athletic coaching practices and cinematic coaching practices to gauge the sports film's potential as a coaching aid. Our analysis suggests the leadership decisions of Norman Dale, fictitious coach of the Hickory High School basketball team in the movie *Hoosiers*, aligns very closely with the five leadership principles and decisions published by Kouzes and Posner. These connections make *Hoosiers*, despite obvious cinematic simplifications, an instructional model for novice and beginning coaches looking to implement transformational and limited transactional coaching practices.

Introduction

Studies of coaching leadership proliferate academic journals devoted to sports psychology, athletic leadership and sport performance (Rangeon, Gilbert, Trudel, & Côté, 2009). One of the most widely accepted leadership approaches is the transformational one set forth by Kouzes and Posner (2002), which proposes five universal leadership principles that exist in any context, including athletics. Though Kouzes and Posner have widely published these five principles in popular literature, the authors ground their theory in more than 20 years of research (Kouzes & Posner, 2002). Several academic studies also utilise the theory, including studies in athletic leadership (Armstrong, 1992; Grandzol, 2011; Grandzol, Perlis, & Draina, 2010). These five principles include: (1) modelling the way; (2) inspiring a shared vision; (3) challenging the process; (4) enabling others to act; and (5) encouraging the heart.

Coaching portrayals in film often depict these methods of leadership and are typically successful in establishing a coach's leadership over a team, producing team cohesion, eliciting successful performances from players and encouraging players to assume their own leadership roles. One such film is *Hoosiers* (DeHaven,

Pizzo, & Anspaugh, 1986), a highly fictionalised account of a small town Indiana high school basketball team's unlikely run to the state championship. The coach in *Hoosiers*, Norman Dale (Gene Hackman), begins as an outsider, establishes himself as the authority figure, wins the support of his players, overcomes the hostility of the fan base and delivers a winning product.

Yet, some argue that the overwhelming success of cinematic coaches such as Norman Dale is the stuff of Hollywood melodrama, not reality. Dale's transformational and transactional leadership abilities strike certain critics as "corny and manipulative" (Schwartz, 2010) and a "naïve masquerade" (Graham, 2007). Film critics are not the only ones to question the overwhelming effectiveness of leadership models like that of Kouzes and Posner. Yukl (1999), while acknowledging that there is "considerable evidence" affirming the effectiveness of transformational leadership, still finds inherent shortcomings such as an overemphasis on dyadic processes and a bias towards the "heroism" of the coach. Other practical circumstances, such as the support of athletic administration, the "buy-in" of players, and the coach's access to, and quality of, facilities, equipment and technology, also alter the effectiveness of Kouzes and Posner's model, supporting the notion that leadership, as portrayed in sports films, may not successfully translate to real-world success. While sports films often allude to these issues, the characters in the films also overcome them quickly and completely.

Yet, even with these minor shortcomings and the apparent ease with which cinematic coaches overcome adversity, many studies in a variety of fields conclude that Kouzes and Posner's five leadership principles effectively gauge both the quality of leadership and the quality of an organisation (Chiok Foong Loke, 2001; Grandzol et al., 2010; Leech & Fulton, 2008; Sumner, Bock, & Giamartino, 2006). Athletic coaches who effectively utilise these principles are, therefore, more likely to be currently building or sustaining quality team cultures. Consequently, finding these five principles in successful cinematic coaches should not be surprising and, in fact, these "celluloid" coaches can function as prototypes for real-life coaches looking to model quality coaching leadership. Analysing Norman Dale's coaching practices in relation to Kouzes and Posner's model in *Hoosiers* will be instructive for coaches, particularly inexperienced and novice ones, attempting to introduce or refine transformative and limited transactional coaching practices into their particular situations and environments.

Model the way

The first principle of Kouzes and Posner's paradigm, Model the Way, argues that effective leaders demonstrate the behaviour they expect from the members of their group. In order to effectively "model the way", leaders should define clear values and convictions in order to set an appropriate example by implementing actions, words and commitments. Highly successful coaches on many competition levels have expressed the ability to "model the way" by both being positive role models for their athletes and intentionally teaching character values (Collins, Gould, Lauer, & Chung, 2009; Gould, Hodge, Peterson, & Petlichkoff, 1987). Effective coaches often exemplify this characteristic by leading altruistically with high character, consistent application of cultural norms and genuine care for their athletes. One study shows that high school coaches who display trust, service and humility typically coach athletes who demonstrate higher levels of self-motivation, satisfaction and athletic mental skills than coaches who do not lead altruistically (Rieke, Hammermeister, & Chase, 2008). Research also suggests that altruistic leadership improves relationships between coaches and athletes (Miller, 2004), which is important for coaches who want to effectively lead their teams (Walsh & Morris, 2002).

Norman Dale's inclusion of two marginalised characters in *Hoosiers* clearly reflects his attempt to "model the way" for his athletes. Through his actions, Dale personally exhibits the trait he most desires his players to emulate: an acknowledgement that every team member is crucial to the success of the team. He first does this with Ollie (Wade Schenck), the smallest and least talented member of the Hickory High School basketball team. The team's view of Ollie as unimportant and, ultimately expendable, is clear during Dale's first practice. Upon Dale's arrival, he notices that there are only seven players and, when he mentions this to the team, Ollie quickly states that there are really only "six and a half" because he is "short and no-good". The editing in the scene highlights the discrepancy between the team's view of Ollie and Dale's view. These aesthetic qualities throughout the film, in emphasising Dale's ideals, act as a "coach" for the audience, guiding the viewer to align with Dale's leadership principles. While relegating himself to the status of "half a player", the film foregrounds Ollie in a medium shot with three of his teammates behind him. Positioning the camera in this way immediately captures the laughter of Ollie's teammates. A cut moves the camera to a medium shot of the remaining three players not in the first shot, who also laugh at Ollie's comments. Finally, the camera shows Dale alone, in a medium shot, not laughing at Ollie, visually setting the coach apart from the players and highlighting the disparate views that each holds of the team. Whereas Dale views each player as an essential cog, the players have created a hierarchy of importance with Ollie on the lowest level possible. Dale's refusal to laugh at Ollie's comments marks his first attempt to "model the way" for his team.

The first practice offers Dale another opportunity to raise Ollie's status to that equal with his teammates. During a passing drill, Ollie is overwhelmed with the speed of his teammates' passing and cannot keep up. This again leads to laughter from the other players. However, Dale's response is more direct than that of the previous scene – the coach tells the players to "wipe that smile off of your face" because "this is not funny". He then begins passing the ball to each of Ollie's teammates while clarifying his objective, which is "five players on the floor function[ing] as one single unit … no one more important than the other". Dale, therefore, demonstrates his belief in team unity and collective importance both physically and verbally during his first practice, effectively restoring Ollie to a position of full team membership.

Norman Dale further models his belief in the power of teamwork by providing Shooter (Dennis Hopper), the town drunk and social outcast, an opportunity to reintegrate himself into society and the game of basketball. In the film, Shooter's habitual drinking has not only separated him from basketball and the townspeople, but also from his son Everett (David Neidorf) who plays on the team. Shooter's alienation stems not only from Shooter's own poor choices, but also from the town's inability to believe that Shooter can overcome what seem to be overwhelming obstacles. More importantly, Dale notices that Everett believes Shooter's troubles are insurmountable, and, therefore, Everett no longer works to help his father overcome these issues. Yet, for Dale, Shooter's troubles are only insurmountable because Shooter is facing them alone; with help, Dale believes Shooter can get sober and contribute to the team and the town.

In order to model the way, Dale recruits Shooter as an assistant coach and provides him with opportunities to contribute through his vast knowledge of basketball. At first, however, Dale's faith that Shooter can recover seems unfounded. When Dale is ejected from a game and passes his playbook to Shooter, the assistant coach remains silent, unable to function in the high-pressure situation. Alternating close-ups of Shooter and Everett highlight the fear of the former and the dejection of the latter. Neither say a word as the timeout, and the game, pass. This apparent failure does not deter Dale. When the assistant coach has an alcoholic relapse, Dale arrives at his house and repeatedly dunks Shooter's head in a tub of water, assuring Shooter that he will not let him quit. In a later game, Dale purposely gets himself ejected in order to provide Shooter with another chance. This time, Shooter overcomes his fear, accepts his role as acting head coach and successfully designs the winning play. To accentuate this growth in Shooter's character, the film inverts the camera angles used in the previous scene. Instead of setting the camera up on Shooter's right, it is now on his left and the close-ups of Shooter and Everett this time capture Shooter's transformation from fearful to excited while showing Everett's shame disappear as he becomes proud of his father. Everett also calms his father's nerves by suggesting a defensive strategy during the timeout instead of remaining silent and passive as he had done in the previous scene. His assistance provides his father with the confidence to proceed and, ultimately, succeed. By following Dale's model of teamwork, Everett realises that Shooter can, indeed, reform his life.

Inspire a shared vision & challenge the process

Kouzes and Posner's second and third principles, to "inspire a shared vision" and "challenge the process", are inter-related. Since the shared future vision coaches wish to inspire is more desirable than the current situation, it follows that groups or individuals must alter current practices or, in some cases, eliminate them.

Therefore, in order to work appropriately to accomplish a shared vision, leaders must challenge the current process by going beyond the comfort level of the group or individuals in the group. Coaches must properly articulate the benefits of the new vision along with the deficiencies of the previous situation, because people are open to changing their culture and vision only if they understand the problems caused by the current culture (Schein, 2004). Both organisational leaders (Cole, 1996; Connors & Smith, 2011) and athletic coaches (Crean & Pim, 2007; Krzyzewski & Phillips, 2000; Pitino & Reynolds, 1997) advocate enacting these principles even though they are often the most uncomfortable in the leadership process.

Norman Dale's vision for the future of the Hickory basketball team connects closely with the principles of teamwork he models. In addition to these philosophical principles guiding Dale's actions are practical applications facilitating Hickory's growth as a team. Many of these applications take place during practice sessions. Coach Dale's emphasis on the fundamentals encourages the type of team play his system demands, fostering collaboration on the court. Similarly, Dale uses actual games to further this "team first" mentality, requiring his players to pass the ball at least four times before shooting during the first game of the year. Similar to his confrontation of Ollie's relegation to "half a player" status, Dale's players do not initially share his vision. Instead, certain players rebel at this challenge to their accepted procedures.

Dale's first practice again provides an example of the coach's vision conflicting with established behaviour patterns. First, Dale interrupts a scrimmage being led by the interim coach, George (Chelcie Ross), and replaces the previously large emphasis on scrimmage with ball-handling and passing drills. Players quickly question this alteration, asking when they will "get to shoot" and complaining that these practices are "no fun". In response, Dale notes that his practices are not meant for the players' enjoyment but to prepare them, mentally and physically, for competition. The film continues to "coach" along with Dale, capturing this exchange between players and coach in a montage sequence, with Dale repeatedly explaining the vision he has for the team as he monitors and facilitates the drills. His comments describe the purpose behind the players' actions. For instance, as Dale follows a pair of players practicing one-on-one defence, he tells them that there is "more to the game than shooting … there are fundamentals and defence". Likewise, Dale makes it known that no team of his "will ever run out of steam before its opponent" as his players run in place and shift their feet at the sound of his whistle. The drills, while not exciting for the players, are meant to produce results that both the players and the coach ultimately desire, and by sharing the importance of the drills with the players, and reminding them about those purposes, Coach Dale is inspiring a shared vision amongst the group.

However, the old visions that the new practices challenge are not easily overcome, and early in Dale's tenure one of the players directly challenges the new vision. At half-time of the first game, after passing at least four times before shooting throughout the first half, Hickory is losing by more than 10 points to their opponent. To start the second half, Rade (Steve Hollar) ignores Dale's instructions, scoring quickly on two consecutive possessions. Dale removes Rade from the game and, challenging normal processes even further, does not re-enter him into the game when another player fouls out, choosing instead to play with only four players. For Dale, the long-term success produced by learning to play as a unit outweighs the short-term success of scoring a few baskets based on individual talent, and his transactional decision to keep Rade on the bench, even when questioned by the fans, players and his assistant coach, serves to cement the new vision.

Dale similarly opposes the actions previously established by the school and the community in his interactions with Jimmy (Maris Valainis), one of the best players in the state who initially does not play on the team because of his grief over the previous coach's death. The other townspeople believe Jimmy is necessary for the team to win, and feel it should be Dale's top priority to convince Jimmy to play again. However, Dale's team-oriented vision does not cater to these notions, and he instead opts to focus his attention on the players who are currently on the team. One scene particularly accentuates this vision and takes place at the pre-season pep rally. After the team, which at the time only has six players, is introduced, the crowd begins to repeatedly chant "We want Jimmy". A slow tracking shot captures the players' faces as they look to each other uncomfortably. Then in another instance of the film "coaching" with Dale, the film cuts to a close-up of Coach Dale's face, recognising the players' emotions, before another cut positions the camera in a long-shot as Dale walks to the microphone. His speech, captured in a medium shot with Dale in the foreground and the players in the background, asks the crowd to accept "who we are rather than who we are not", and ends with a cut to a slightly wider angle, bringing the players into clearer focus, with Dale pointing at them and saying "This is your team". The editing and framing of the scene contrast with the earlier practice scene described above which separated the coach from the players. This scene visually represents Dale's vision to unify the entire team. Therefore, his refusal to recruit Jimmy both develops his vision of a team functioning as a collective unit willing to sacrifice themselves for each other, and challenges the preconceived expectation and vision of the townspeople.

Enable others to act

Once the aspiring leader begins to challenge the status quo of the group, the Kouzes and Posner model then suggests the leader "enable others to act". In this phase of leadership, the leader must focus on developing trust between leaders and followers and encouraging cooperation between all members of the organisation. Several qualitative studies of coaching leadership behaviour note this as a necessary component to team success (Collins et al., 2009; Mead, 2015; Miller, 2004). Part of this aspect of leadership is encouraging certain athletes to take leadership responsibility on the team. The delegation of leadership responsibilities is practical, pragmatic and effective. Research indicates that athlete-leaders can influence both task and social cohesion (Vincer & Loughead, 2010) and that athletes are much more effective than coaches at influencing this social cohesion (Moran & Weiss, 2006; Price & Weiss, 2013). As a result, part of a coach's leadership should be to "enable others to act" by encouraging and developing leadership characteristics among athletes on their team.

Previous examples have already indicated how Coach Dale's modelling of leadership characteristics led to leadership from other characters. Dale's faith in Shooter, for instance, and his insistence on Shooter's worth to the team provided the assistant coach with an opportunity to lead while also giving Everett an opportunity to follow Coach Dale's model. Additionally, Dale's conviction that Ollie is just as important to the team as the other players provide an opportunity for a player to take leadership action. In the state tournament semi-finals, two players foul out and one player gets injured, forcing Ollie to enter the game with Hickory winning by four points with under one minute to play. Ollie proceeds to dribble to ball off of his leg and out of bounds on the team's next offensive possession, and then air ball a free throw on the subsequent possession. Thanks to Ollie's dismal play, Hickory's opponent scores five quick points and takes a one point lead with little time remaining. With time running out and the other team purposely leaving Ollie unguarded, the little guard picks up a loose ball and gets fouled as he attempts a desperation heave. Ollie is verbally bullied while waiting to shoot his free throws as an opposing player tells him that he "didn't know they grew them so small on the farm". These words recall Ollie's own words of degradation during the first practice when he and the team believed that he was not worthy to be considered a full player. However, based on the shared vision of teamwork and mutual importance produced throughout the season, Ollie's teammate Merle (Kent Poole) approaches Ollie and tells him "not to worry about that" and instead, "just concentrate on what" he is doing and "put them in the hole". Instead of outwardly expressing doubts in Ollie's ability to perform, Merle speaks to Ollie as if he is fully capable of making the free throws, treating him as a peer. Ollie then makes both free throws, sending Hickory to the championship game. Like Everett speaking to and believing in his father, Merle follows Dale's vision that team members, working together, can overcome any obstacle. Dale's vision, both visually and verbally modelled throughout the season, creates opportunities for players to act in a manner consistent with that vision.

Another example of player leadership takes place during the championship game. With the score tied late in the fourth quarter, Hickory steals the ball and calls a timeout. During the stoppage, Coach Dale devises a play to use the star player, Jimmy, as a decoy in order to free up another player for the potential game winning shot. Dale's words are met with a hesitant silence from the players, and he quickly realises that something is wrong. As opposed to his demands that the players adhere to his commands "without question" early in the season, Dale asks the players about their problem with his play call. Jimmy, looking in Dale's eyes, tells the coach that he will "make it". Dale allows the players to have their way, and allows Jimmy to take the last shot, which he makes. Dale's acceptance of the team's wishes and enabling of Jimmy's leadership role acknowledges the shared vision that the entire team now holds. Not only are the players enabled to act as leaders, but Dale is also able to show servant leadership, a quality much connected with transformational leadership success as well as higher levels of player motivation, task cohesion and satisfaction (Rieke et al., 2008). Dale continues to model effective leadership practices even during the last game, and in the process enables his players to take leadership roles they were in no position to take early in the season.

Encourage the heart

Finally, leaders should consistently "encourage the heart" by genuinely celebrating successes and contributions of individuals and groups as they occur. Positive feedback is often regarded as a preferred leadership behaviour among athletes (Chelladurai, Haggerty, & Baxter, 1989). Also, athletes tend to be more satisfied (Riemer & Chelladurai, 1995; Weiss & Friedrichs, 1986) and have greater team cohesion (Shields, Gardner, Bredemeier, & Bostro, 1997) when their coaches provide more positive feedback and social support. Coaches, though, tend to have different approaches to genuine celebration and positive feedback based on the age of the athlete and the competitive level of the sport (Jambor & Zhang, 1997). For example, coaches of team sports with strong individual components offer more positive feedback than coaches of team sports with greater team interdependency (Schouten, 2011). Despite the research indicating that social support, positive feedback, and some level of democratic decision-making is beneficial, coaches are much less likely to "encourage the heart" of their athletes in these ways than peer athletic leaders (Loughead & Hardy, 2005; Moran & Weiss, 2006).

Coach Dale occasionally utilises positive feedback to encourage his team and highlight solid play. One example takes place during the first game that Shooter attends as assistant coach. The players, beginning to play well as a unit and reaping the benefits of successful team play, have a substantial lead over their opponents. During a timeout, Dale tells the team they are "playing real well, real well", while also encouraging them to tighten up their defence and be "more patient on offense". His acknowledgement of their success further emphasises the importance he has placed on teamwork all season long. Now that the team is utilising his methods and succeeding, Dale's acknowledgement encourages the players to continue working together to that end.

The most overt example of verbal encouragement takes place during Dale's pre-game speech prior to the semi-final. He tells his players the following:

> Forget about the crowds, the size of the school, their fancy uniforms, and remember what got you here … focus on the fundamentals we've gone over time and time again … and most importantly, don't get caught up in thinking about winning or losing this game … if you put your effort and concentration into playing to your potential, to be

the best that you can be, I don't care what the scoreboard says at the end of the game, in my book you are going to be winners.

Ultimately, Dale tells his team their success or failure relates not to their win and loss total, but to their growth as teammates and adherence to hard work and skill development. His speech further solidifies the notion that unification has been his primary goal, and his reiteration of this to his players before their most important athletic contest reminds them their worth is not caught up in their success on the scoreboard, but in whether they fulfil their collective potential.

When not using overt positive feedback, Coach Dale also "encourages the heart" of his team through other means. An example of this takes place as the team arrives for practice before the state championship game. As Hickory enters the large stadium where they will play the championship game, the size of the facility visibly overwhelms. To ease their anxiety about the stadium, Dale takes out a tape measure, has the players measure the distance from the basket to the free throw line and then the height of the basket above the floor. When the players read the measurements as fifteen feet and ten feet, respectively, Dale says, "I think you will find those exact same measurements in our gym back in Hickory". This visual demonstration provides his players with the confidence that, no matter where they play, who they play or how many people are watching, when working collectively they can compete with any other team.

Conclusion

In *Hoosiers*, Norman Dale's leadership exemplifies the five attributes proposed by Kouzes and Posner (2002), and his decisions at critical junctures during the season enable his team to have a highly successful season. Yet, while the movie is very loosely based on a true story and Dale's leadership can be used as an example for real-life coaches to follow, it is often the case that leadership is not as clean and perfect as this film's presentation for several reasons. First, film-makers alter and edit cinematic representations of events, even those based on reality, to enhance the viewing experience for a majority of patrons. Motivational speeches almost always result in improved athletic performance, even though there is research indicating that inspirational motivation from coaches does not directly relate to increased athletic effort (Arthur, Woodman, Ong, Hardy, & Mtoumanis, 2011). Likewise, there are many other factors that influence athletic success other than coaching leadership, but athletic films rarely mention the role that talent or administrative oversight has on winning or losing. For example, a high school team forced to rely on a player with the talent level and playing experience of Ollie often would not win a contest when facing opponents of higher skill sets. Also, some of Dale's transactional methods, including removing two players from practice his first day on the job and refusing to enter a fifth player after another fouls out, are not always met with the administrative support Dale is provided.

Second, the nature of most sports films requires the condensing of several months' time into less than two hours, so movies eliminate or downplay many of the struggles a coach would encounter implementing transformational and transactional leadership during the season. Studies also indicate that coach–athlete compatibility (Kenow & Williams, 1999) and athlete narcissism (Arthur et al., 2011) influence the ability of a coach to lead a team, but films also quickly resolve these situations due to time constraints. For example, the situation with Jimmy choosing not to play in *Hoosiers* begins and concludes within several scenes, and Jimmy transforms from a character refusing to play basketball into someone who will only play for Coach Dale. Likewise, the two players removed from the first practice of the season return to the team later in the film, and Rade, who overtly challenged Dale's methods during the first game, also adheres to the coach's vision with no further incidents after "thinking it over" for one weekend.

Despite these obvious departures from the realities of coaching, the principles laid out in the character of Norman Dale can provide a ground work for coaches looking to establish their own leadership and provide others with the opportunity to lead. Dale refused to allow players or the surrounding community to alter his vision, and he modelled and inspired a vision for a culture that esteemed every member of his team. He honoured his commitments to that culture and enforced his values in all circumstances, which eventually resulted in player acceptance of the culture and internal peer leadership. This led to increased team cohesion and, ultimately, team success. Finally, Dale clearly ties his vision of success with his vision of team unity instead of the game's final score. In these ways, even when not exactly duplicating reality, sports films can provide leadership lessons applicable to athletic coaches, particularly when their cinematic counterparts, like Norman Dale, display the five principles laid out in Kouzes and Posner's work.

Disclosure statement

No potential conflict of interest was reported by the authors.

References

Armstrong, S. (1992). *A study of transformational leadership of athletic directors and head coaches in selected NCAA division III colleges and universities in the midwest* (doctoral dissertation). Retrieved from ProQuest Dissertations and Theses. (Accession Order No. AAT 9310069)

Arthur, C. A., Woodman, T., Ong, C. W., Hardy, L., & Mtoumanis, M. (2011). The role of athlete narcissism in moderating the relationship between coaches' transformational leader behaviors and athlete motivation. *Journal of Sport & Exercise Psychology, 33*, 3–19.

Chelladurai, P., Haggerty, T. R., & Baxter, P. R. (1989). Decision style choices of university basketball players and coaches. *Journal of Sport & Exercise Psychology, 11*, 201–215.

Chiok Foong Loke, J. (2001). Leadership behaviours: Effects on job satisfaction, productivity and organizational commitment. *Journal of Nursing Management, 9*, 191–204.

Cole, L. (1996). *Frustration is your organization's best friend: Measuring corporate culture change*. Conway, AR: LifeSkills.

Collins, K., Gould, D., Lauer, L., & Chung, Y. (2009). Coaching life skills through football: Philosophical beliefs of outstanding high school football coaches. *International Journal of Coaching Science, 3*, 29–54.

Connors, R., & Smith, T. (2011). *Change the culture, change the game: The breakthrough strategy for energizing your organization and creating accountability for results*. New York, NY: Portfolio/Penguin.

Crean, T., & Pim, R. (2007). *Coaching team basketball: Develop winning players with a team-first attitude*. New York, NY: McGraw-Hill.

DeHaven, C. (Producer), Pizzo, A. (Producer), & Anspaugh, D. (Director) (1986). *Hoosiers (Motion Picture)*. USA: Orion Pictures.

Gould, D., Hodge, K., Peterson, K., & Petlichkoff, L. (1987). Psychological foundations of coaching: Similarities and differences among intercollegiate wrestling coaches. *The Sport Psychologist, 1*, 293–308.

Graham, P. (2007, March 21). Hoosiers. Retrieved August 4, 2015, from http://www.chicagoreader.com/chicago/hoosiers/Film?oid=1060516

Grandzol, C. J. (2011). An exploratory study of the role of task dependence on team captains' leadership development. *Journal of Leadership Education, 10*, 57–70.

Grandzol, C., Perlis, S., & Draina, L. (2010). Leadership development of team captains in collegiate varsity athletics. *Journal of College Student Development, 51*, 403–418.

Jambor, E. A., & Zhang, J. J. (1997). Investigating leadership, gender, and coaching level using the Revised Leadership for Sport Scale. *Journal of Sport Behavior, 20*, 313–321.

Kenow, L., & Williams, J. M. (1999). Coach–athlete compatibility and athlete's perception of coaching behaviors. *Journal of Sport Behavior, 22*, 251–259.

Kouzes, J. M., & Posner, B. Z. (2002). *The leadership challenge* (3rd ed.). San Fransisco, CA: Jossey-Bass.

Krzyzewski, M., & Phillips, D. T. (2000). *Leading with the heart: Coach K's successful strategies for basketball, business, and life*. New York, NY: Warner Books.

Leech, D., & Fulton, C. R. (2008). Faculty perceptions of shared decision making and the principal's leadership behaviors in secondary schools in a large urban district. *Education, 128*, 630–644.

Loughead, T. M., & Hardy, J. (2005). An examination of coach and peer leader behaviors in sport. *Psychology of Sport and Exercise, 6*, 303–312.

Mead, J. (2015). *Leadership development of high school varsity basketball captains with mentoring by their coach* (Unpublished doctoral dissertation). Northern Illinois University, Dekalb, IL.

Miller, L. M. (2004). *Qualitative investigation of intercollegiate coaches' perceptions of altruistic leadership* (doctoral dissertation). Retrieved from ProQuest Dissertations and Theses. (Accession Order No. AAT 3124373)

Moran, M. M., & Weiss, M. R. (2006). Peer leadership in sport: Links with friendship, peer acceptance, psychological characteristics, and athletic ability. *Journal of Applied Sport Psychology, 18*, 97–113.

Pitino, R., & Reynolds, B. (1997). *Success is a choice: Ten steps to overachieving in business and life*. New York, NY: Broadway Books.

Price, M. S., & Weiss, M. R. (2013). Relationships among coach leadership, peer leadership, and adolescent athletes' psychosocial and team outcomes: A test of transformational leadership theory. *Journal of Applied Sport Psychology, 25*, 265–279.

Rangeon, S., Gilbert, W., Trudel, P., & Côté, J. (2009, June). *Coaching science in North America*. Paper Presented at the 12th ISSP World Congress of Sport Psychology, Marrakesh, Morocco.

Rieke, M., Hammermeister, J., & Chase, M. (2008). Servant leadership in sport: A new paradigm for effective coach behavior. *International Journal of Sports Science and Coaching, 3*, 227–239.

Riemer, H. A., & Chelladurai, P. (1995). Leadership and satisfaction in athletics. *Journal of Sport & Exercise Psychology, 17,* 276–293.

Schein, E. H. (2004). *Organizational culture and leadership.* San Francisco, CA: Jossey-Bass.

Schouten, J. (2011). *Leadership behaviors of athletic coaches in the Council for Christian Colleges and Universities* (doctoral dissertation). Retrieved from ProQuest Dissertations and Theses. (Accession Order No. AAT 3458722)

Schwartz, D. (2010, June 3). Hoosiers. Retrieved August 4, 2015, from http://homepages.sover. net/~ozus/hoosiers.htm

Shields, D. L., Gardner, D. E., Bredemeier, B. J., & Bostro, A. (1997). The relationship between leadership behaviors and group cohesion in team sports. *The Journal of Psychology, 131,* 196–210.

Sumner, M., Bock, D., & Giamartino, G. (2006). Exploring the linkage between the characteristics of it project leaders and project success. *Information Systems Management, 23,* 43–49.

Vincer, D., & Loughead, T. M. (2010). The relationship between athlete leadership behaviors and cohesion in team sports. *The Sport Psychologist, 24,* 448–467.

Walsh, J., & Morris, T. (2002). The perceptions of expert coaches about effective leadership in sport. *Journal of Science and Medicine in Sport, 5,* 93.

Weiss, M. R., & Friedrichs, W. D. (1986). The influence of leader behaviors, coach attributes, and institutional variables on performance and satisfaction of collegiate basketball teams. *Journal of Sport Psychology, 8,* 332–346.

Yukl, G. (1999). An evaluation of conceptual weaknesses in transformational and charismatic leadership theories. *The Leadership Quarterly, 10,* 285–305.

The traditional, the ideal and the unexplored: sport coaches' social identity constructs in film

Sue Jolly and John Lyle

School of Sport, Leeds Beckett University, Leeds, UK

ABSTRACT

The sport coaching construct within mainstream fiction films has been described as stereotypical, reinforcing the traditional notion of the sport coach as a technician who conquers all, or a hapless individual, open to ridicule from athletes and fans. Although this depiction is also prevalent in some independent fiction films and documentaries, film sub genres such as social realism and "fly on the wall" style documentaries move away from the "Hollywood sports film structure" towards stories that focus on everyday coaching moments. Through a critical discourse analysis of two U.K. films (*Bend it Like Beckham* and *Twenty Four Seven*), both featuring sport coaches in central roles, we reflect critically on these mass media multidimensional representations in terms of the sport coaching professionalisation agenda in the U.K. and the social identification process of sport coaches within their sporting environments.

Introduction

In this paper, we examine the identity portrayal of sport coaches in two independent U.K. films (*Bend it like Beckham* and *Twenty Four Seven*). Although fictional and based on the directors'/screenwriters' notions of what sport coaching means to them, the sport coach characters have the potential to propagate an image that reinforces or challenges that being described by academic writers on the professionalisation of coaching, or reflects the narratives of the majority of sport films, depicting the sport coach as a mechanism to achieve a utopian dream (Crosson, 2013). Acknowledgement of how media, and in particular film, portrayals of sport coaches invoke or ignore emerging concepts of sport coaching is central to the professionalisation debate. Awareness of such depictions may prompt the policy community in sport coaching to consider critically how these portrayals contribute to the development of coaching as a valued profession. They also offer sport coaches an opportunity to self-reflect on these sometimes stereotypical representations by comparing and contrasting their own perceptions with those of the directors/producers (Hills & Kennedy, 2013).

Gilbert and Côté (2013) have reclassified a number of conceptual and theoretical frameworks into one overarching framework, proposing three types of knowledge – professional, interpersonal and intrapersonal. These different perspectives attempt to delimit professional knowledge but, more importantly, form the basis of a conceptualisation of professional practice that is evident in the coach's behaviour. Sport coaches' professional knowledge has been situated in everyday social interactions within particular contexts (Cassidy, 2013; Cushion, 2011; Jones, 2009). In most of this work, there is an implicit link between the development of knowledge and the social construction of the sport coach's identity. In other words, implicit within professional knowledge construction (description, categorisation and process) is an assumed meaning related to sport coaches' identity construction. This is a contested arena and ripe for further study. In the context of this study, the meaning we attach to social identity construction and by default professional knowledge is influenced by Jenkins' (2014) ideas on social identity.

Jenkins describes social identity/ identification as a function of both the individual and the collective; "it's how we know who's who and what's what" (2014, p. 14). It is a process rather than a set of characteristics that we possess. For Jenkins, therefore, knowledge construction is an implicit part of the process of social identification. Social identity can be described in terms of three categories that are interlinked and time-dependent; the individual order (the world of embodied individuals and what goes on in their heads), the interaction order (the world of co-presence and relationships between embodied individuals, what goes on between people), and the institutional order (the world of patterned, organised and symbolically templated ways of doing things) (Jenkins, 2000, p. 5). In terms of sport coaching knowledge and social identification within films, we will be cognisant of the meaning of sport coaching identity as constructed through the social interactions and storylines, the process of character building, how the directors show their interpretations of coaching through the everyday interactions within the plot, and the patterns and symbols within sport that appear to have influenced them.

Hills and Kennedy (2013) go some way towards exploring the notion of everyday coaching practice. However, their comparisons were mainly concerned with mainstream Hollywood films and coaching behaviours evident in youth coaching. There are no studies that explore the British sport independent film genre in relation to sport coaches' identity constructs. This paper aims to address this issue via a critical discourse analysis (CDA) of two films – *Bend it like Beckham* and *Twenty Four Seven*.

Independent films are a specific genre of films. Genre refers to the film's form; for example, the style of narrative cinematography and sound, and the way that the directors play with these elements leads to specific conventions within particular film genres. The independent film genre in Britain has a long history, in which sport has played an important role, tackling issues including national identity, regionalism and cultural conflicts, particularly within a working-class setting, in films such as *The Flying Scotsman, Mike Bassett, When Saturday Comes* and *Bend it Like Beckham*. These films have borrowed from the narrative arch of the Hollywood sports films – sport's capacity to resolve different social issues (Rowe & Lawrence, 1998). Alongside social realism and new British realist films, there is a sub-genre of independent films that challenge the more formulaic model of narrative found in mainstream independent films. These films focus on the struggles of everyday life, painting a bleaker picture of society. They are recognisable by a more adventurous narrative and cinematography style, typically borrowing from art house methods of production. [For example, see *This Sporting Life, The Loneliness of the Long Distance Runner, Kes, Looking for Eric* and *Twenty Four Seven.*] Although the production process may at first appear to be insignificant for the analysis of sport coaching constructs, Scott (2013) illustrates how the genre of new British realism and the DIY production process have produced an in-depth ethnographic style that has the capacity to explore people's "lived experience".

The sport coach construct in British sport films – The *traditional* notion of the coach

In most of the coaching-related British independent films, the coach could be described as either the hapless, comedic character, a figure to be made fun of or the stereotypical coach/instructor who spend his time shouting instructions from the sidelines to "motivate" his team. The former is portrayed in the film *Kes*:

> Ken Loach's poignant 1969 classic Kes features coach Brian Glover taking a rather sadistic session for the boys at his school. Glover likens himself to Manchester United great Bobby Charlton in scenes that seem to stick in the memory for many football fans and film buffs. (Metcalfe, 2014).

Robert Carlyle's portrayal of an ex-football player who is now coaching the local football team in *There's only one Jimmy Grimble* demonstrates the latter.

The film and media research associated with analyses of this genre of film tends to analyse it in terms of the sub-plot, that is, the relationship between sport and society. For example, Crosson (2013) and Babington (2014) focus on the links between sport and national identity. The coach's role is analysed, if at all, in terms of this broader perspective, not in terms of the construction and portrayal of the sport coaches' sport identity, which is not treated as a problematic theme.

Bend it like Beckham and *Twenty Four Seven* have each been a focus for analysis for media researchers. Studies on the former have highlighted the link between transcultural issues and race within contemporary Britain (Rings, 2011). In these, the coach is critiqued in terms of his national identity in relation to the national identity of the main protagonist Jess. The analysis of the coach also links the characters' storyline and construction to the typical Hollywood male narrative.

There is no reference to the coach's role within sport or the link between everyday coaching skills and practice in relation to construction of the coach's identity. Godfrey (2013) also analyses at length the character of Darcy in *Twenty Four Seven*. Her work focused on the link between masculinity and loss of this in 1980s Britain, in a context of political tensions.

Hills and Kennedy (2013), however, do address the relationship between everyday coaching behaviours and the coach's representation within society. In their research, they explore the link between the evidence-based coaching styles displayed in effective practice in youth sport and the coaching styles represented in sport films. They analysed three Hollywood mainstream films, demonstrating how the constraints of the "Hollywood" formulaic treatment of the mainstream sports film led to stereotypical representations of coaches. The coaches displayed "Hollywood masculinity", a character profile that leaves no room for realistic coaching styles to be part of the identity construct.

The characterisation of sport coaches as authoritarian and self-focused has been used in polemical portrayals of "traditional" styles of coaching as a critical reference point against which to encourage more "enlightened" practice (Kidman, 2005). There is a corpus of writing in coaching that portrays this traditional style of delivery as reflecting and reinforcing power hierarchies and expectations in an unproblematic and unconsidered way (e.g. Potrac & Jones, 2011).

The professionalisation agenda, professional knowledge and the *Ideal* notion of the coach

There is a professionalisation agenda within the sport coaching policy network that is focused on improving the status of sport coaching and developing an occupation with a distinctive body of knowledge that is evident in education and training, and an ethical framework (Duffy et al., 2011; Lyle & Cushion, 2010). The recent interest in the professionalisation of sport coaching has been well-documented (Duffy et al., 2011; ICCE, 2013; Taylor & Garratt, 2010, 2013). Much of the literature is aspirational and idealised. Duffy et al. (2011) argue that there is opportunity to evolve the current landscape for coaches in the U.K. and internationally, to increase the quality of sport coaching practice and its status. The U.K. Coaching Framework (Sports Coach UK, 2008) and the International Framework for Coaching Excellence (ICCE, 2013) outline similarly idealistic visions. These proposals identify the need for coaching systems building and include reference to an evidence-based body of knowledge that will be applicable to a diverse range of sporting environments. Such documents are aimed at sport coach policy-makers and administrators, acting as a reference point for their coaching systems building roles. This led to national sport organisations offering "ideal" coaching practice scenarios to support their education programmes. In some instances these come in the form of *You Tube* clips of sport coaches in staged coaching settings. These clips offer a prescribed and what may be interpreted as an ideal way to coach.

Taylor and Garratt (2010) believe that there is resistance to this construction of the coach identity described by the policy-makers.

Much of the debate about professionalisation remains aspirational and is conducted largely within the sport coaching community itself. There is limited evidence, if any, of a drive towards profession status from the public's perception of the coach's role or contribution to social priorities. In addition, the documents referred to above have an element of "moral high ground" about them. Unsurprisingly, they promote a set of ethical behaviours and practices that may not be evident in much of coaching practice. We speculate that media representations of the coach are unlikely to reinforce the idealised conception of coaching emanating from the coaching policy network.

Method

The purpose of this paper is to conduct a critical analysis of two films and to document the depiction of the coach's role therein. We chose two British independent sport films in which coaches play a pivotal role to the plot. These were purposefully chosen to reflect differences and similarities within the identity construct of the coach.

We accept that our personal perspectives about professional knowledge and what it means to be a coach will undoubtedly influence the process; attempting to minimise this bias by recognising the complexity associated with classifying professional knowledge. We chose not to use one theoretical framework to guide the data collection; rather we will remain cognisant of all the different perspectives. High-level terms associated with professional knowledge act as reference points during the analysis process; for example, coaching behaviours and communication, sport-specific technique, tactical decision-making, planning and pedagogy, coaching communication and emotions and self-reflection. We use a concurrent inductive and deductive analysis process similar to McCarthy and Jones (2007).

Sue watched each of the films three times, took notes and coded the transcripts. She also analysed selected interviews with the directors and the actors playing the coaches, in addition to sampling purposefully film reviews from established British film critics. We chose CDA as the analysis tool, adopting Fairclough's (2010) conceptualisation of CDA, in which text is always analysed in relation to both other texts and social contexts. It involves three elements, "text, discursive practice and social practice" (Sparkes & Smith, 2014, p. 138). We were aware of both the strengths and weaknesses of this method of analysis, including those arising from our position of power within the research process, and the tendency to analyse the deconstruction of text, as opposed to both deconstruction and reconstruction. The latter process is more likely to bring out positives and negatives within the analysis, while also highlighting the lack of multiple voices represented; for example, audience reception.

To counteract these weaknesses in the analysis technique, we make our position as interpreters explicit, self-reflecting on our own interpretations and our use of language and by acknowledging our position of power as authors. To address a lack of multi-voice representation, we have used Hall's Reception Theory (1980) to guide the film and media analysis. This involves including opinions of film-makers, actors and film critics about the film's meanings. We focus on the film-making process to highlight the impact this has on the film's storyline and content.

A brief outline of the film storylines is as follows:

Bend it like Beckham The story is about an Indian girl Jess, who is obsessed with playing football, but her family do not approve of girls playing football and would rather she settles down and married a nice Indian Boy. Unbeknown to her parents, Jess joins the girls' local football team and with the encouragement of her coach, Joe, and her best friend Jules, and after many trials and tribulations, she is encouraged to confront her parents and carry on playing football, in order to help the team win the league and to gain a scholarship to the USA.

Twenty Four Seven Darcy, a middle aged man from a typical working class town in Nottingham, decides to try to help the lads of the estate, to give them a chance to break free from a life with no hope. He sets up a boxing club and through the boxing, the lads go on a journey of discovery about themselves. Darcy sets up a public fight, which gets all the community involved to prove that they can do something. However, as the fight date gets closer, the lads' confidence wanes, which leads to disastrous consequences.

The stereotype – *Bend it like Beckham*

The first scene with Joe, the coach: he is a handsome figure, dressed in a tracksuit and long overcoat, the football "uniform" that is common amongst managers in British professional football. Logos displaying information about sponsors are emblazoned on the tops and trousers. He is watching a training session, which is conducted on a football training ground that is well resourced. All the girls are in pristine football kit. Initially, no eye contact is made when he speaks to Jess and Jules; he appears withdrawn and slightly non-plussed about the whole situation, as if he's going through the motions.

Coach: I want two groups of three in each group. Let's move! – How do you know she's serious? I haven't got time to piss around Jules.

Jules: She's got balls, Joe. – At least watch her.

Jess: Hi.

Coach: Where do you normally play?

Jess: In the park.

Coach: I mean what position?

Jess: Sorry! I usually play all over, but up front on the right is best.

Coach: Get your boots on.

Jess: I haven't got any.

Coach: Right, join in. Start warming up.

Here the coach uses familiar instructional techniques and, at the same time, adopts an informal but aloof manner to both connect with and control the situation. His sullen disposition is used to build up our knowledge of his past; a past that includes "failures" in football due to injury, the ex-athlete turned to coaching, a typical storyline of the Hollywood masculine sports film (Crosson, 2013).

Coach: Are your folks up for it?

Jess: Yeah, they're cool.

Coach: Suppose you'd better come back, then. I've got to go and open the bar. Some real work!

Jules: He likes you.

Jess: You think so?

Jules: He asked you back, didn't he? – How long have you been playing?"

The coach is now interested in Jess. He can see that she can play, and because of this, his manner softens. He is more engaged in the conversation, offering eye contact and checking that it is okay with her parents for her to play football. Here is the reference to Jess's Indian upbringing, rather than the introductory routine that he carries out when first meeting new potential players. There are no formal introductions, no managing of expectations, an interaction process that might be expected in a structured community sport club/school environment. At a societal level, the writer Chadha briefly touches on the status of community sport in the U.K. Joe references the fact that he has to do "real work", in the bar, indicating that he is a volunteer coach for the girls. This topic is revisited at the end of the film when Joe is offered a more "prestigious" job of coaching the junior boys team, which, to complement the film's overall message, he turns down.

In the remaining scenes within the film, the coaching dialogue between Joe and Jess was largely superficial, and there were limited examples of social identification. The dialogue and scenes with Joe appeared more to do with building up the romantic storyline than a reflection of athlete /coach interactions. Although we do not deal with it here, the romantic liaison storyline between athlete and coach is an example of the ethical dimensions of sport coaching and an issue for the professionalisation agenda.

Joe's communication style with the rest of the football squad appears to have an informality about it that we recognise in everyday communications between individuals who have developed respect and trust over time. For example, there are both non-verbal and verbal communication patterns that are part of everyday social interactions and some that we recognise as "football" culture. We ourselves have experienced this in schools, local clubs and within the media; the unwritten "way things are" within that particular sporting environment (Jenkins, 2000,

2014). These portrayals of traditional expectations are also present to a lesser or greater extent in other British sporting films of this era; for example, *Fever Pitch*, *When Saturday Comes* and *There's only one Jimmy Grimble*.

In terms of the core features of professional knowledge, Joe did exhibit interactions that could be described as humour, empathy, instruction, naturalistic decision-making, some self-reflection and impression management. Although these limited snapshots of Joe's coaching interactions could be accused of being successful and representational or "superficial" and stereotypical; nevertheless, they were present.

In her interviews, Chadha, the writer, acknowledges that she has fond memories of sport through her father's interest in cricket, and this was her "research" of the sporting world. To some extent, therefore, there is a quasi-autobiographical thread running through the film. Although sport and the sport coach's role is the plotline mechanism for the film, the real story, that of a strong independent Indian girl dealing with transcultural issues, highlights the emotional connection to the "language" of sport in society. We speculate, therefore, that in relation to the coach's identity and the professionalisation agenda, there may be losses as well as gains if the emerging "ideal" coaching discourse and implicitly adopted practices replace the stereotypical mainstream media representation of the coach.

The unexplored – *Twenty-four seven*

Darcy, the coach, is the central character of the film. He narrates his own life story through his experiences as a coach in the boxing club he has set up to help the "lads" of the housing estate. The whole film is shot in black and white; the music score purposefully chosen, not only to represent the times and the minor moments in the film, but also to evoke the continuous sense of dissolution and abandonment that is core to the plot. The opening frames see a young man helping another older man out of a derelict shelter on a railway track. He is obviously in a bad way through alcohol misuse. He takes him back to his house, cleans him up and puts him to bed. You later realise that the old man was Darcy, the coach. The audience's first introduction to him is in stark contrast to the coach in *Bend it Like Beckham*.

We are then taken back to five years earlier. These scenes slowly build up the characters by focusing on the relationship between Darcy and the "lads", highlighting in a subtle way how much knowledge the coach had about the participants' backgrounds and their upbringings. There is no distinction between sporting and coaching knowledge, and insights into their backgrounds. It is all integrated and useful to him. Darcy, through his narration continually self-reflects and by doing so reveals his coaching and life philosophies. He uses this knowledge to make decisions about how he responds to each of the boys; how to motivate them to join the club and how to keep them motivated. These insights, plus the knowledge of how Darcy was coached as a young person, influence his technical coaching and relationship building. When hearing that Fagash is to appear in court, he pleads with the judge to give him another chance:

> Listen off the record, you were around when the boxing club ran when we were kids, you know yourself what happened, the crime rates went down, we had something to believe in, these lads are all survivors, let them fight within the ring, give them, give Fagash just one more chance.

Using the pace of the film, writer Shane Meadows depicts how the engagement/recruitment process takes time; it is not an immediate, implicit or taken-for-granted action. Unlike most sports films and in *Bend it like Beckham*, the film does not rely on the usual sporting codes and stereotypes. Rather, Meadows appears to reject them outright. In fact the film enters the boxing arena and shows the act of technical coaching only one third of the way through the film. In other scenes Darcy is seen "life" coaching, trying to teach the lads discipline and respect. He has a natural, kind disposition, in the main he is softly spoken, although at times his emotions get the better of him. The idea of coaching the person as well as technique is a recognisable and interrelated act; a message that is emphasised within the professionalisation agenda by numerous sports coaching researchers (Jones, Armour, & Potrac, 2002; Potrac, Jones, Purdy, Nelson, & Marshall, 2013).

The coach continuously uses the contextual knowledge he has acquired through his own lived experience on the estate. His communication techniques and his behaviour management skills are at times in keeping with his upbringing and the environment. The boys understand and expect an element of "tough love"; this is not "out of keeping" with what they are used to receiving from their families and mates. They appear to be grateful that someone cares. The social interactions highlight what Jenkins (2014) terms as practices of identification that "allow us to navigate through the world that is intrinsically uncertain". These "coaching" acts, therefore, could be said to be a contextualisation of sophisticated coaching knowledge. However, they could also be seen as inappropriate and "unprofessional" behaviour, especially for those who have not been exposed to the nuances of the context. Although there are times when Darcy shows subtle communication techniques, there are also times when it could be said that he reverted to coaching behaviours that he himself had experienced. Jenkins (2014) describes this as primary identification, the environment and social interactions that are developed in the formative years, and influence social interactions throughout life.

Darcy's character is also subtly developed throughout the film. Initially, he is portrayed as a bit of an eccentric, someone everyone knows around the estate – harmless but open to ridicule and gossip. His coaching "uniform" is not typical of a coach. In one scene, he returns from the toilet in a tight fitting white and grey tracksuit with a large pair of leather boots. This is not conventional, but the "lads" do not care. This is in stark contrast to Joe in *Bend it Like Beckham* who looks more like a "professional coach" and appears to have the respect of his team and the community from the beginning of their interactions.

The coach is also portrayed as a kind, proud and sometimes lonely man, who uses coaching to fill a void and to give hope for a better life to himself as well as the "lads". As the film develops, he loses a sense of perspective and this degenerates to the condition witnessed in the opening sequences. This has a strong element of social realism (Godfrey, 2013).

In terms of the sport coach's social identity, Darcy's resolution for the social and personal deprivation is to be nostalgic, to harp back to a time that was happy and supported and worked in his life. The coach's role in those times replicated in parts the role of a father, a person who was there, maybe not *Twenty Four Seven*, but certainly one who was around informally when needed. This stable presence is in contrast to current initiatives in community sport coaching, in which agencies are temporary and have limited connection to the community, which militates against the building of relationships (Houlihan & Green, 2011; Mason, 2015).

Discussion

To some extent *Bend it like Beckham* paints a picture of the comfortable stereotype, overplayed perhaps, but non-threatening and demonstrating application of both sport-specific and delivery knowledge. This was in obvious contrast to the flawed but good-hearted intentions of Coach Darcy. During the analysis, we became attached to *Twenty Four Seven*, and in particular the character of Darcy. We admired the way Meadows had rejected the stereotypical representation of the sport coach, in favour of a man who despite his circumstance evidenced a subtle level of intelligence that is normally not present in the depiction of working-class people in sport films. We resonated with the space and people, but it also made us reflect on what might be appropriate professional practice in this context. We were drawn to the slightly romantic vision of Britain in the 1980s that Meadows refers to in his interview; nostalgia for a changed community (Godfrey, 2013).

The films' representation of the sport coach was dictated to some degree by the genre. There is no doubt that Meadows has pushed the boundaries of the social realism genre to become more like an ethnographic film (Scott, 2013). This opens up possibilities for similar portrayals of sport coaching moments. Sport and recent music documentaries have crossed the boundaries between fact and fiction, with directors using novel ways to tell stories, stories that could not be told if the directors were to adhere to the traditional documentary making techniques. Such a formula has the potential to offer accounts that probe more deeply into the past and everyday lives of their subjects. This could be an unexplored tool for self-refection and research from which sport coaching could benefit. As Hills and Kennedy (2013) recognised in her cinematic exploration of sport coaches, the film in any guise has potential to be a teaching tool, and if the teaching tool is rich in everyday coaching moments, this has even more potential.

The traditional, the ideal and the unexplored are categories relating to social identity that not only resonate with media portrayals and assumptions but provide a framework for further enquiry into what is a contested field of study. There is a distinction between the social phenomenon that is coaching, with its observable behaviour, shared interpretations and meanings and social esteem and performance-based expertise. There are also competing ideologies with a (perceived) traditional authoritarianism and unproblematic replication of knowledge criticised by more context-dependent and athlete-centred approaches.

We have to recognise that the subtlety of performance-related contextual practice is unlikely to be represented in film, and using the coach as a vehicle to explore social issues may present a danger of the coach's practice itself becoming superficial. Although this may be an opportunity to treat stereotypical practice as problematic, this may not be possible with an uninformed audience. On the other hand, the treatment of Darcy, the unexplored, gave the audience the story behind the image presented, and there was a greater implicit examination of the contextual factors in his story. Sport coaching may be paying the price of being a hidden profession (Lyle & Cushion, 2010). The advantages of enhanced visibility through film characters may be negated by stereotypical representations of the coach in the search for, and reinforcement of, a social identity. The "ideal" may be promoted via education and development, but more varied and realistic sport coaching characters may demonstrate how the individual's social identity is shaped by layers of context.

Exploring these films has highlighted the process of knowledge construction and the contextualisation of the core features of professional knowledge. This has given a new perspective on the symbiosis between professional knowledge and professional identity. It has demonstrated that types of knowledge and emphasis on different components ebb and flow between moments and within contexts. Being "professional" appears to mean both different and similar things to the various sporting communities; the researchers and professionals, the fans and general public and the mass media and ourselves. What this exercise has highlighted to us is that both the deliberate and inadvertent depiction of coaches needs to be part of the professionalisation debate.

Disclosure statement

No potential conflict of interest was reported by the authors.

References

Babington, B. (2014). *The sports film: Games people play*. London: Wallflower Press.
Cassidy, T. (2013). Holistic sports coaching: A critical essay. In P. Potrac, W. Gilbert, & J. Denison (Eds.), *Routledge handbook of sports coaching* (pp. 172–184). Abingdon: Routledge.
Crosson, S. (2013). *Sport and film*. Abingdon: Routledge.
Cushion, C. (2011). Coach and athlete learning: A social approach. In R. Jones, P. Potrac, C. Cushion, & L. T. Ronglan (Eds.), *The sociology of sports coaching* (pp. 166–178). Abingdon: Routledge.

Duffy, P., Hartley, H., Bales, J., Crespo, M., Dick, F., Vardhan, D., & Curado, J. (2011). Sport coaching as a 'profession': Challenges and future directions. *International Journal of Coaching Science, 5*, 93–123. Retrieved from http://www.ikcdc.net/

Fairclough, N. (2010). *The Routledge handbook of discourse analysis*. Harlow: Longman.

Gilbert, W. D., & Côté, J. (2013). Defining coaching effectiveness: A focus on coaches' knowledge. In P. Potrac, W. Gilbert, & J. Denison (Eds.), *Routledge handbook of sports coaching* (pp. 147–160). Abingdon: Routledge.

Godfrey, S. (2013). 'I'm a casualty, but it's cool': 1990s British masculinities and Twenty Four Seven. *Journal of British Cinema and Television, 10*, 846–862. doi:http://dx.doi.org/10.3366/jbctv.2013.0183

Hall, S. (1980). Encoding/decoding. In S. Hall, D. Hobson, A. Lowe, & P. Willis (Eds.), *Culture, media, language: Working papers in cultural studies 1972-79* (pp. 128–138). London: Hutchinson.

Houlihan, B., & Green, M. (2011). *Routledge handbook of sports development*. Abingdon: Routledge.

Hills, L., & Kennedy, E. (2013). Ready, set, action: Representations of coaching through film. In P. Potrac, W. Gilbert, & J. Denison (Eds.), *Routledge Handbook of sports coaching* (pp. 40–52). Abingdon: Routledge.

ICCE/ASOPIF/Leeds Metropolitan University. (2013). *International sport coaching framework Version 1.2*. Champaign, IL: Human Kinetics.

Jenkins, R. (2000). Categorization: Identity, social process and epistemology. *Current Sociology, 48*, 7–25. doi:http://dx.doi.org/10.1177/0011392100048003003

Jenkins, R. (2014). *Social identity* (4th ed.). Abingdon: Routledge.

Jones, R. (2009). Coaching as caring ('The smiling Gallery'): Accessing hidden knowledge. *Physical Education and Sport Pedagogy, 14*, 377–390. doi:http://dx.doi.org/10.1080/17408980801976551

Jones, R. L., Armour, K. M., & Potrac, P. (2002). Understanding the coaching process: A framework for social analysis. *Quest, 54*, 34–48. doi:http://dx.doi.org/10.1080/00336297.2002.10491765

Kidman, L. (2005). *Athlete-centred coaching*. Christchurch: Innovative Print.

Lyle, J., & Cushion, C. (Eds.). (2010). *Sports coaching: Professionalisation and practice*. Edinburgh: Churchill Livingstone.

Mason, W. (2015). Austerity youth policy: Exploring the distinctions between youth work in principle and youth work in practice. *Youth and Policy, 114*, 55–74. Retrieved from http://www.youthandpolicy.org/wp-content/uploads/2015/04/yandp114.pdf

McCarthy, P., & Jones, M. (2007). A qualitative study of sport enjoyment in the sampling years. *The Sport Psychologist, 21*, 400–416. Retrieved from http://www.humankinetics.com

Metcalfe, N. (2014, April 2). Golden years: From bobby, pele and best to Jossy's Giants, when saturday comes and Beckham in only fools and horses... when the beautiful game has been at the movies and on the tele. Retrieved July 2015, from http://www.dailymail.co.uk/sport/football/article-2593523/Football-movies-TV.html

Potrac, P., & Jones, R. L. (2011). Power in coaching. In R. L. Jones, P. Potrac, C. Cushion, & L.T. Ronglan (Eds.), *The sociology of sports coaching* (pp. 135–150). Abingdon: Routledge.

Potrac, P., Jones, R. L., Purdy, L., Nelson, L., & Marshall, P. (2013). Coaches, coaching and emotion. In P. Potrac, W. Gilbert, & J. Denison (Eds.), *The Routledge handbook of sports coaching* (pp. 235–246). Abingdon: Routledge.

Rings, G. (2011). Questions of identity: Cultural encounters in Gurinder Chadha' s Bend it Like Beckham. *Journal of Popular Film and Television, 39*, 114–123. doi:http://dx.doi.org/10.1080/01956051.2010.541954

Rowe, D., & Lawrence, G. (Eds.). (1998). *Tourism, leisure and sport: Critical perspectives*. Melbourne: Cambridge University Press.

Scott, J. (2013). From local roots to global screens: Shane Meadows' positioning in the ecology of contemporary British film. *Journal of British Cinema and Television, 10*, 829–845. doi:http://dx.doi.org/10.3366/jbctv.2013.0182

Sparkes, A., & Smith, B. (2014). *Qualitative research methods in sport, exercise and health: From process to product*. Abingdon: Routledge.

Sports Coach, UK. (2008). *The UK coaching framework*. Leeds: Author.

Taylor, W. D., & Garratt, D. (2010). The professionalisation of sports coaching; relations of power, resistance and compliance. *Sport, Education & Society, 15*, 121–139. doi:http://dx.doi.org/10.1080/13573320903461103

Taylor, W. D., & Garratt, D. (2013). Coaching and professionalisation. In P. Potrac, W. Gilbert, & J. Denison (Eds.), *Routledge handbook of sports coaching* (pp. 27–40). Abingdon: Routledge.

Filmography

Barron, S., & Peplow, S. (2001). *Mike Bassett: England Manager*. United Kingdom: Entertainment Film Distribution.

Chadha, G. (2002). *Bend it like Beckham*. United Kingdom: Rank Film Distribution.

Daly, J., Lambert, C., & Teper, M. (1996). *When saturday comes*. United Kingdom: New Line Cinema.

Garnett, T., & Loach, K. (2009). *Kes*. United Kingdom: United Artists.

Hay, J. (2000). *There's only one Jimmy Grimble*. United Kingdom: Pathé distribution , Front Row TV.

Mackinnon, D. (2007). *The flying scotsman*. United Kingdom: Verve Pictures.

O'Brien, R., & Loach, K. (2009). *Looking for Eric*. United Kingdom: Icon Film Distribution.

Posey, A., & Evans, D. (1998). *Fever pitch*. United Kingdom: Phaedra Cinema.

Reisz, K., & Anderson, L. (1963). *This sporting life*. United Kingdom: Rank Organisation, Janus Films.

Richardson, T. (1962). *The loneliness of the long distance runner*. United Kingdom: Continental.

West, I., & Meadows, S. (1998). *Twenty four seven*. United Kingdom: Pathé.

Mind the gap: female coaches in Hollywood sports films

Katharina Bonzel

College of Arts and Social Sciences, Australian National University, Canberra, Australia

ABSTRACT

In the summer of 2015, the NFL employed both their first female professional referee and their first female coach, while the NBA now has two female coaches in its employment. Representations of female coaches in contemporary popular sports films are, however, virtually non-existent. No mainstream sports film has featured a female coach as a central character since 1996. The overwhelming majority of sports films are about male coaches coaching male athletes. Women coaching men, in particular in professional sports, remain an often uncrossed boundary in films about coaching. This study analyses the depiction of female coaches in three Hollywood films – *Wildcats* (1986), *Eddie* (1996) and *Sunset Park* (1996) – arguing that while these films may well have feminist intentions, they overwhelmingly conform to stereotypical and essentialist ideas of the "woman as coach" trope.

Introduction

2015 proved to be a remarkable year for female coaches in American professional sports: not only was the number of professional coaches in the National Football League (NFL) and National Basketball Association (NBA) increased from one to three (plus an added professional referee in the NFL), but Becky Hammon, an assistant coach with the San Antonio Spurs, became the head coach for the summer league and led her team to the title. Yet, most of these were only temporary positions. In 2016, the NFL team Buffalo Bills added the first female full-time professional coach to their roster: Kathryn Smith is now the quality control assistant coach on special teams. Despite these advances, women coaching men or men's teams is still a rarity. This is perhaps less surprising when one considers women's coaching involvement in sport more generally. According to Vivian Acosta and Linda Jean Carpenter, whose longitudinal study "Women in Intercollegiate Sport" has monitored, amongst other things, coaching opportunities for women between 1977 and 2014, the number of female head coaches of men's teams has only had a "negligible increase" and remains very low at between 2 and 3.5% (Acosta & Carpenter, 2014, p. 18).[1]

In professional sports, hires like Amelie Mauresmo as a coach for tennis star Andy Murray provoked an outburst of gendered, mostly sexist, commentary. The press coverage of this "event" ranged from "Mauresmo's natural warmth and sensitivity were evident" to "Andy Murray gets his girl guide Amelie Mauresmo before Wimbledon."[2] The limitations of hiring practices for coaches, however, does not only impact female coaches, as a recent study on racial diversity in the NFL showed. While minorities make up 67% of players, only 6 out of 32 teams have minority coaches (Rider, Wade, Swaminathan, & Schwab, 2016). Thus, white male coaches remain the dominant force in leadership positions within the sport of American football.

Sports as represented in popular narrative films are as gendered as in reality and, surprisingly, reality is ahead of Hollywood for once – professional female coaches of men's teams are very hard to come by in Hollywood sports films. *Eddie* (Steve Rash, 1996), a Whoopi Goldberg comedy, is the only high-profile sports film to feature a female coach of a professional men's team, in this case the New York Knicks basketball team, defying both gender and racial biases. When it comes to coaching non-professional sports, for example high school, we can add the Goldie Hawn comedy *Wildcats* (Michael Ritchie, 1986) and the drama *Sunset Park* (Steve Gomer, 1996). Yet women athletes on screen, from the track and field stars in *Personal Best* (Robert Towne, 1982) to boxer Maggie Fitzgerald (Hilary Swank) in *Million Dollar Baby* (Clint Eastwood, 2004), are regularly coached by men.[3] Films with female athletes coached by men also often depict the coaching of women as the lowest rung on the coaching ladder, as seen, for example in *Bend it Like Beckham* (Gurinder Chadha, 2002) and *Believe in Me* (Robert Collector, 2006) thus devaluing female sports. In *Bend it Like Beckham*, these preconceptions are turned on their head when the male coach rejects an offer to coach the men's team in favour of staying with the girls team. While this appears to be a well-intentioned trope in sports films with male coaches of female teams, this suggests that even the validation of women's sports remains in the hands of men. The scarcity of sports films with female protagonists is in and of itself telling, and has been noted by a range of scholars (Babington, 2014; Baker, 2003; Chare, 2015; Crosson, 2013; Lieberman, 2015; Poulton & Roderick, 2008; Tudor, 1997), but what are we to make of the virtual non-existence of the female coach – since *Eddie* in 1996, no major Hollywood film has featured a female coach of male athletes?[4]

This paper argues that the differences in the depiction of female and male coaches visually and narratively demonstrate how hegemonic gender roles are both created and upheld by the Hollywood sports film. As Italian philosopher Antonio Gramsci argued, power is maintained by both coercive forces and ideological control and cultural hegemony thus works to obscure oppression by the ruling classes through constructing norms and belief systems that appear to be obvious (Gramsci, 1992). These belief systems, however, are not inherently stable, and it is in this context that Seán Crosson (2013) contends that "sport, film and media more generally play a central role both as a means of maintaining hegemonic power but also as sites revealing the tensions inherent in its maintenance" (p. 5). It is precisely these tensions that sports films with female coaches lay bare only to then conceal them again as if frightened by their own bravery. As much as films with female coaches such as *Wildcats* and *Eddie* thematise the gender of the coach to legitimise their professional capacity, and, ultimately, seek to validate the "woman as coach" trope, they often undermine this seemingly progressive, even feminist, endeavour by adhering to an essentialist understanding of gender differences. That is to say, these films are heavily invested in the idea that there are indeed innate, biological differences between men and women, which have a direct influence on their skills and social behavior. When, for example, women are seen as less aggressive and competitive than men, this essentialist understanding of women translates directly to their ability, or rather *in*ability, to coach. In particular, this article puts forth three key differences between female and male coaches, which demonstrate how these well intentioned films are in fact strengthening the hegemonic gender order both within and beyond the professional sporting world, much to the detriment of women's equality.

Firstly, in these films, the competence of female coaches is either continually questioned or is a main strand of the narrative, thus giving it excessive attention. This contrasts starkly with the representation of male coaches in films such as *Coach Carter* (Thomas Carter, 2005), where convention dictates that the coach's competence or newfangled strategy is briefly questioned, only to have this quickly contained and sealed by a big win. Secondly, gaining the respect of the players is fraught with tension and elicits highly gendered responses – where male coaches mostly assert their authority over male players by either physical or verbal aggression,[5] female coaches gain authority by diverse strategies: on the one hand, displays of physical bravado and stamina to show they are "one of the boys," but at the same time, a motherly understanding and nurturing of the players. This "mothering" of the female coaches contributes to the third strategy these films employ: the desexualising of the female coaches. This final strategy limits the perceived threat to the hegemonic order posed by a woman who holds power over men in her capacity as coach.

To illuminate the problems that these characters pose to hegemonic social order, I draw on George Mosse's influential study *Nationalism and Sexuality* (Mosse, 1985). Mosse argues that the rise of modernity and the nation state coincided with the birth of "ideal manliness" – a concept that, ultimately, sought not only to prescribe the roles and norms of masculinity, but also of femininity; of normality and deviance; and of the "other". In order to guarantee the stability of the nation, everyone was assigned his or her role in society:

> Alongside the idealization of masculinity as the foundation of the nation and society, woman, often accused of shallowness and frivolity, was at the same time idealized as the guardian of morality, and of public and private order. (Mosse, 1985, p. 17)

Mosse's work on gender and sexuality in the modern nation state offers important insights into why female athletes, for example, have long been a contested site for the (in)flexibility of gender boundaries. Athleticism in women is permitted only up to a point, as many scholars have pointed out, before the transgression becomes an apparent threat to the stability of established gender norms, which in turn underlay the heteronormative structures of family, community and nation. Heroines operate within strictly policed gender boundaries, conforming to what Tuttle (1988) calls a "feminizing code" to ensure the femininity of female athletes – the etiquette and appearance guideline of the All American Girls Baseball League, for example, as featured in *A League of their Own* (Penny Marshall, 1992) (p. 10).[6] As J. Thompson writes of the literary heroine, "[s]he is required to be both heroic – superior or exemplary in some way – and female – inferior by definition", a characterisation that Jennifer Hargreaves productively applies to the sporting heroine, whom she argues must combine seemingly opposing characteristics of kindliness and competition, or strength and caring (quoted in (Hargreaves, 2000, p. 2)).

The female coach, while not an athlete by definition, is nevertheless "tainted" by her association with sports, a world still very much governed by men. This was especially so in the 1980s and 1990s, in which period the three films examined here are set. In these films, showcasing women making their way in a "man's world," the social equilibrium – succinctly summarised by Mosse (1985) as "[m]an was active and woman passive, and the two roles must not be confused" – is disturbed (p. 17). The female coach's femininity and role in society are openly negotiated, and the tension brought on by her transgression of normative gender roles is palpable.

The problem of women as coaches

Molly, a girl can't coach football, you know that. (Coach Dan in *Wildcats*)

All coaches on film have to, at least to some degree, prove their competence for the job. Female coaches, however, face much harsher scrutiny than their male colleagues. In *Coach Carter*, for example, the namesake of the film simply points to his name on the Hall of Fame board in the gym and announces to his new team that his record-setting credentials are there for all to see. It is only one line of dialogue in a long opening speech by the coach, and the topic does not come up again during the film. In *Eddie*, *Wildcats* and *Sunset Park*, on the other hand, each of which features a female coach, competence for the job is not only frequently mentioned, but also forms a distinct strand of the narrative. On the surface, these films make a seemingly good-willed effort to legitimise women as coaches for their audiences: they are represented as knowledgeable and capable of the role, despite what their male players, employers, fellow coaches or fans of the team might think. Yet, the films' dogged and visible insistence on the fact that these female coaches are as qualified as male coaches marks this as something that needs to be proven in the first place. The effect is dissatisfying, and, ultimately defeats ostensible attempts to normalise female coaches.

Two films, *Eddie* and *Sunset Park*, mark their protagonists initially as either willfully incompetent (*Sunset Park*) or out of their depth (*Eddie*). In *Wildcats*, the coach's incompetence is simply assumed by the players, despite indications to the contrary. In all three films, this initial suggestion of incompetence constitutes the original narrative tension that these characters must overcome, as they prove their abilities to players and employers alike. This is a careful balancing act, for in each case, the audience is left in little doubt of the character's actual competence for the role, or that, in true Hollywood style, this will be resolved by the end of the film. Yet, this overt narrative tension also hides a larger, unspoken tension with regard to women in positions of power over men. These are, moreover, not just any men, but all-American male athletes: whether high school stars or NBA millionaires, in a North American context these are the heroes of our day.

In *Eddie*, Whoopi Goldberg plays the title character Edwina "Eddie" Franklin, a die-hard New York Knicks fan, who wins the chance to be "fan coach" for the night – a publicity stunt by new owner "Wild Bill" Burgess (Frank Langella). The boisterous Eddie proves to be a success with the other fans, especially as she clashes with the actual coach, John Bailey (Dennis Farina). Wild Bill, seeing the team as a means to make money regardless of sporting success, fires Bailey, who has a million dollar contract, and instead hires Eddie for a mere $50,000, regardless of her lack of coaching experience at an elite level. While Eddie is shown to successfully coach an inner-city boys' team, and it is clear that she knows the Knicks inside out, it is equally clear that she knows nothing about professional coaching. Only once she gains the trust and respect of the team do they begin a winning streak that takes them all the way to the playoffs. It is a film that thematises gender, but it is also film for fans of the Knicks, and for fans everywhere, showcasing their power to shape the direction of their beloved team.

Competence in *Eddie* is marked as essential for the team, the coach and the fans – in other words only within the *sport* of basketball. For the team's owner, a disciple of the Gordon Gekko "greed is good" school of capitalism, competence is irrelevant as long as Coach Eddie raises attendance at the games, and thereby increases revenue. Eddie is not only a "woman coach", but a loudmouthed, black working-class woman coach at that, raising questions about the intersectionality of race, class and gender in the film.

In *Sunset Park*, Brooklyn teacher Phyllis Saroka (Rhea Perlman) takes on the coaching of her school's male and predominantly black basketball team. Unlike Eddie, she does so not out of a fundamental love for the sport, but to earn extra money to pursue her dream of opening a restaurant. Disinterested in both the boys and basketball, she lets the team effectively coach itself until one of the boys accuses her of coaching only for the paycheck. From then on she throws herself into studying basketball coaching and learning the intricacies of the sport from the team leader, Shorty Doo-Wop (Fredro Starr), whose pragmatic willingness to help out is rooted in his love for the game. The team improves both because of Phyllis's increasingly shrewd coaching and their growing belief in her – and their own – abilities. The latter is not only part of a longstanding trope in sports films – evident, for example, in films such as *Hoosiers* (David Anspaugh, 1986) and *Coach Carter* – but also reflects a broader trend toward "white savior" narratives in US films dealing with race: once the white person deems his or her charges worthy and shows his/her belief in them, they suddenly believe in themselves and start improving their lot (Hughey, 2014). After Phyllis intervenes in several of her players' personal problems, from being bullied by a teacher to being charged with a gun crime, the team reaches the city championship. Despite a narrow loss, Phyllis gives up her dream of owning a restaurant and instead promises to continue coaching the team.

In *Wildcats*, Goldie Hawn plays idealistic girls' track & field coach Molly McGrath, daughter of a famed football coach, who dreams of coaching high school football. When she is overlooked for the coaching job of the junior varsity football team at her prestigious private school, she instead goes off to coach the senior football team at an underprivileged inner-city high school. Despite being vilified by her team at first, Coach Molly proves her mettle and eventually gains the trust of her charges and leads them to the city championship, including a rousing final win over her former school. Further heightening the tension in the already gendered narrative, a sub-plot about her custody battle for her two daughters challenges Molly's suitability as a mother while coaching a boys' football team.

Competence, respect, authority and power

In each of these three films, the lead character is at first seemingly marked as lacking the ability to fulfill her newfound role – or rather, she is viewed as unqualified by many of those around her. This framing serves to divorce sports knowledge and coaching experience – which each of the characters is shown to possess, at least to an extent – from the question of competence. Instead, the latter is equated with the gender of the coach: in each case, it is the coach's femaleness that prevents her from being considered a capable coach of male athletes. For example, in *Wildcats*, Molly McGrath finds out that she has been tricked out of becoming the junior varsity football coach at her school, and that the job has gone to the stereotypically nerdy male home economics teacher. A not-so-subtle gender role inversion is at work here: through his association with a "feminized" school subject and with his nerdish, somewhat effeminate outer appearance, the home economics teacher presents as the emasculated polar opposite to Molly, with her tomboyish sportiness and restrained femininity. Yet biological sex wins out over actual competence, and he is given the job.

Molly's football competence is clearly on display in a meeting with the principal, the home economics teacher and the senior varsity coach, Dan Darwell (Bruce McGill), when she rattles off a series of questions at the hapless new coach concerning a variety of football plays and strategies. Yet despite his obvious incompetence, Molly stands no chance. When she asks the football-specific question

"What about penetration? Do you know how to get good penetration?", both the principal and the home economics teacher start shifting uncomfortably in their seats and the principal answers: "Ms McGrath, please, we're drifting off the subject now!" Misreading "penetration" as a sexual act, in what is clearly also intended as comic relief for a particularly tense moment, the two men interpret Molly's question as a direct critique of the home economics teacher's masculinity, and thus his ability to coach football. Despite her being portrayed by America's sweetheart Goldie Hawn, this awkwardly turns Molly into an uncomfortable phallic woman, signified by her knowledge of penetration.[7] Molly, within the logic of the film, has enough masculinity to coach, and her knowledge of football marks her as a threat to the vulnerable masculinities around her. The film thus shows off the sexism at work in the coaching world, but rather than fully supporting its protagonist, the scene devolves into a joke on Molly.

Head coach Dan Darwell then informs Molly that instead of junior varsity, she can teach varsity football at Central High, a school that the principal objects to as "not a place for a woman." Dan then taunts Molly: "She can handle it, can't you, Molly? Besides, maybe a woman's touch is just what they need ...". Molly, infuriated, tries to put the men in their place by retorting: "I'm gonna take that job. You think a woman can't be tough enough? I'll show you tough! Watch me!" The men are stunned into silence and Molly leaves with her head held high. The effect of this feminist statement should be empowering, but is ultimately undermined. Rather than ending the scene at the point when the men look at each other uncomfortably, thus signaling both their wrong-doing and their recognition of it, Molly sheepishly returns to pick up her purse. This dissolves the previous tension by re-associating Molly with a symbol of femininity lest she be too threatening to the men around her – or, indeed, to the audience in the cinema. This comic resolution showcases humour as a key strategy in defusing the "gender wars" surrounding the figure of the female coach on film.[8]

In *Eddie*, this same sexist assumption of incompetence is on display when Eddie Franklin first starts coaching the Knicks. Indeed, even Eddie herself insists that she cannot coach an NBA team, but is convinced by Wild Bill Burgess to continue. After her first loss as the new coach, the film cuts to a vox pop by a local news reporter, who asks the "pundits on the street" their opinion of the new coach. Invariably, the answers range from non-committal to insulting: "It's a joke, it's an embarrassment – a woman coach!" Eddie's lack of success in coaching the team – the players mostly ignore her – seemingly proves the pundits right. Yet once Eddie has gained the trust and respect of the team, using strategies examined below, they find themselves on a winning streak. At this point, the vox pop scene is mirrored; now, however, the male pundits have changed their mind on the competence of the female coach. Unlike *Wildcats*, *Eddie* does not undermine its protagonist directly, even though her gender leads her qualifications to be questioned at first. As a result, Eddie's competence, once established, stays intact.

Phyllis Saroka is greeted by her team with the words "I *know* we gonna lose every game now" when she introduces herself as the new coach. *Sunset Park* at first gives credence to the belief that "women can't coach", but Phyllis is not beyond redemption – indeed, once she throws herself into learning the game, she becomes a great coach, as is pointed out by one of her players in an emotionally charged scene where his full disappointment about her plans to leave the team and open a restaurant with the extra cash from the coaching job comes to the fore: "Well, you ain't so perfect either. You're a *great* coach an' you don't even know it. That's how stupid you are. I thought you wanna be great at somethin': you're a great coach!" The typical montage scenes of the team's improving performance are intercut with shots of Phyllis' rising interest in basketball and coaching. These scenes of Phyllis buried in basketball books, or watching games and instructional videos, signal two important developments. Firstly, these scenes undermine coaching as a professional occupation that requires training and experience, and secondly, they unnecessarily gender the learning process, suggesting that girls learn by reading and boys by doing.

These scenes demonstrate how the films in question tie the question of coaching competence to gender, and, in doing so overtly thematise it. This contrasts with most sports films featuring male coaches, where competence is usually only briefly mentioned, as in the aforementioned example of *Coach Carter* – a male coach comes, it appears, with innate sports coaching competence. The narrative tension created by this apparent gendered misalignment is crucial to each of these films, masking the underlying, and significantly more threatening, problem of women assuming power over men. As June Sochen succinctly states, "since the dominant cultural values assume that all major power positions have been, and therefore, should be occupied by men, it remains unusual, exceptional, and unique to see women in central roles of power in American life and film." (Sochen, 1993, p. 98) Thus gaining the respect of, and the authority over, the players, is both of particular significance and complexity for Eddie Franklin, Phyllis Saroka, and Molly McGrath.

While male coaches in typical Hollywood sports films frequently gain respect by verbally or physically abusive means and threatening power plays that showcase their authority over their players, female coaches are more likely to gain respect by demonstrating how much pain (physical or emotional) they themselves can take. In *Remember the Titans* (Boaz Yakin, 2000), a film about the racial tensions in a newly integrated high school football team, Coach Boone (Denzel Washington) first publicly humiliates and then bullies the white star players when they come to him with demands for the white players on the team. After calling them Jerry Lewis and Dean Martin in front of the team and the parents as they are boarding buses for the team camp – a reference which marks their demands as the joke of a comedy duo, and which is aimed at ridiculing them – Boone explains:

> Once you get on that bus you ain't got no Mama no more. You got your brothers on the
> team, and you got your Daddy. Now, you know who your Daddy is, don't you? Gerry, if

you wanna play on this football team, you're gonna answer me when I ask you: Who's your Daddy? Who's your Daddy, Gerry?

This dialogue is softly spoken, but all the more threatening for the tension it produces through the obvious humiliation of Gerry, who lowers his eyes and almost cowers like a puppy before the alpha dog. In *Coach Carter*, by contrast it is physical abuse that gains Coach Carter the respect of the team: he slams an unruly player, who tries to hit him, into the wall of the gym. When the student protests that "teachers ain't supposed to touch students," the coach replies with an icy "I'm not a teacher. I'm the new basketball coach." These kinds of power plays are effectively turned on their head in the films discussed here. Instead of the female coaches being abusive themselves, they are subjected to abuse, both physical and verbal, by their alleged charges.

In *Wildcats*, Coach Molly McGrath's office is vandalised and sprayed with vulgarities, and her first meeting of the team is an exercise in sexual harassment aimed at humiliating and intimidating her: when Molly enters the locker room, her team is dressed only from the waist up. The players are holding their helmets in front of their genitals and then simultaneously put the helmets on their heads with the words "We're suited up and ready to play, Coach." As Megan Chawanksy rightly points out, this scene shows that the "team has struck early, clearly marking their territory and sending the message: the phallus rules in this locker room." (Chawansky, 2010, p. 173) Discussing gendered spaces in the context of nineteenth-century Paris, Griselda Pollock has argued that

> [The spaces of femininity] are the product of a lived sense of social locatedness, mobility and visibility, in the social relations of seeing and being seen. Shaped within the sexual politics of looking they demarcate a particular social organization of the gaze which itself works back to secure a particular social ordering of sexual difference. (Pollock, 1988, p. 66).

The spaces of masculinity, conversely, are equally embedded in these social relations, and the principal's warning "that is no place for a woman" is given visual credence here – the locker room is decidedly not to be viewed as a feminine space. The hierarchies at work here are slowly eroded throughout the rest of the film, with Molly eventually claiming the locker room as *her* space by ignoring her players' protests and inhabiting it, eventually, with the confidence gained through her performance as coach.

Finally, Molly has to prove her sporting credentials by outlasting the entire team in a running contest before they will allow her to coach them. However, this power struggle is short-lived. Once Coach McGrath shows she can outrun her players, not only is the coach–player hierarchy restored, but the reversal in power is accompanied by growing mutual affection as Coach McGrath becomes something akin to the mother figure of the team. I discuss this process of desexualising the coach and instead turning her into an untouchable mother figure in more detail below.

Coach Franklin in *Eddie* and Coach Saroka in *Sunset Park* suffer a similar, if less dramatically abusive fate: at first the teams simply ignore them, or taunt them verbally: "You can't coach, Miss! Face it! Why don't you just quit?," asks one of the players in *Sunset Park*. Eddie, much like Coach McGrath, resolves the issue of authority through physical means, by taking a hit from one of the more antagonistic players in order to demonstrate a defensive play. This display of toughness – despite being knocked down much more aggressively than is necessary she continues to concentrate on explaining the defensive play – finally gains her the respect of the rest of the team. It is not so much her knowledge of rules, strategies or team members' athletic performance that effects this shift, but her willingness to take physical pain for the team. It is as much an exercise in male posturing as it is a denial of the coach's femininity – a direct confrontation that physically removes the gendered obstruction to her ability to coach this team. By becoming "one of the boys" through physical punishment, they afford her with the privilege of coaching them. Coach Saroka, on the other hand, makes a deal with the players: they will teach her basketball, and she will use her smarts and experience to help them win.

There are two distinct, but equally significant aspects of these highly gendered interactions between the coach and players. Firstly, aggression and dominance is coded as masculine. Secondly, when the female coaches finally do gain respect and authority, they do so at the players' discretion. The usual power balance of coach over athlete is reversed in these films until the players decide differently – the power is theirs to give. Thus power, framed in terms of dominance, still resides with men. Unlike female athletes, who through their sheer physical power and incompatibility with stereotypically feminine traits disrupt hegemonic gender norms and threaten the social order, female coaches reach for symbolic power. The many narrative strands of power – who has it, who doesn't? – turn into a Gordian knot, which is ultimately cut decisively by the sword of hegemonic masculinity. This is similar to the way in which the film *Bend it Like Beckham* validates its footballing girl power heroines Jess (Parminder Negra) and Jules (Kiera Knightley) through their fathers, as Justine Ashby asserts: "when each father finally puts his foot down and insists that their wives support their daughters' ambitions, the fathers strike a blow for "girl power," on the one hand, while reasserting their more traditional power as head of the family, on the other." (Ashby, 2005, p. 130) *Sunset Park*, *Wildcats* and *Eddie* actively defuse the threat of the female coach by marking her power as temporary and conditional on male approval: it is not hers to begin with, and thus can potentially be revoked at any time. To further rein in the unruly femininities these coaches represent, the films employ a different strategy: that of desexualisation.

Desexualising female coaches

Hey Coach, can I ask you a question? Say, if you was a girl ... Shorty Doo-Wop

I AM a girl! Coach Saroka (*Sunset Park*)

Other films of this era featuring powerful women, such as *Disclosure* (Levinson, 1996), about a female executive sexually harassing a male subordinate or *Working Girl* (Nichols, 1988), about a secretary unveiling the ruthless idea-stealing schemes of her female boss, equate, as Tasker (1998) puts it, "working women, women's work and some form of sexual(ised) performance." (p. 3) These films explicitly sexualise their protagonists, albeit in different ways. *Disclosure* presents Meredith Johnson (Demi Moore), the new manager at an IT firm after the hero Tom (Michael Douglas) has been overlooked for promotion, as an executive-*femme fatale* hybrid, who actively uses her sexuality to move ahead. In contrast, Tess (Melanie Griffith) in *Working Girl* is shown to be frustrated by her constant sexualisation, both at home by her boyfriend and at work by her male bosses.

Quite in contrast to these films, in which the anxieties created by women attaining (or seeking to attain) power are directly linked to the highly sexualised characterisation of their protagonists, sports films from the 1980s and 1990s featuring female coaches desexualise their main protagonists once they have gained authority over their male players. Indeed, the female coaches become the "mother" of the team, symbolising a shift from sexual object and potential predator towards a domesticated, almost asexual femininity. This shift is an important strategy in ensuring the stability of social order, for Mosse (1985) points out that "the roles assigned to [woman] were conceived of as passive rather than active. She was to be a guardian, protector, and mother" (p. 17). All three films employ these tropes in their depiction of the female coach during her transformation from a sexual object to desexualised figure of authority.

This shift is particularly noticeable in *Wildcats*. During the power struggle between Coach McGrath and her team, one of her players "talks trash" about her:

> Well, I hope she stays 'cause I figure I only got a few more days 'til I get my hands on her. Look, she knows I got ten pounds of danglin' fury just waitin' for her. Shit, I know she wants it.

As Chawansky (2010) argues in her analysis of the misogynist and homophobic rhetoric in the locker rooms in *Sunset Park* and *Wildcats*:

> [h]is tone positions McGrath not as a subject or an authority figure, but rather as an object in a heterosexual fantasy that he controls. To be able to control her in this capacity far outweighs any control she may exert as the head coach of the football team on which he plays (p. 173).

This aggressive behavior, which seeks to assert the superiority of the male players over their female coaches, is surprisingly easily reversed. Once Coach McGrath has earned their respect by outrunning them, no further aggression, verbally or physically, touches the coach. Instead, the players start feeling protective of her, which several scenes demonstrate. For example, during the party after the team's first win of the season at Coach McGrath's house, her ex-husband shows up and, in an attempt to speak to Molly, he grabs her arm and pulls her towards him. Immediately a player struts to her side saying aggressively: "Don't be grabbin' the Coach like that!" Later in the film, the players show up to court as character witnesses, as Molly is fighting a custody battle with her ex-husband over their two daughters. While well intended, their support for Molly backfires as they are deemed too rough an association for Molly's young girls and she has to either quit coaching or lose custody during the football season. Regardless of the outcome of the custody battle, these scenes demonstrate a complete reversal of their initial hostility and sexual aggression towards Molly. Molly, on the other hand, guards the moral virtue of her young charges by, for example, refusing to let them drink alcohol, trying to censor their language and inspiring them to be less selfish. That this is successful is evidenced in their attempt to help her with her court case.

Eddie Franklin, while not subjected to the kind of sexual harassment that Molly faces, is also desexualised. From the start, Eddie is only ever seen in baggy clothing, ranging from ill-fitting men's suits for her job as a chauffeur to New York Knicks fan garb worn over bulky sweaters. These costumes are clearly chosen to de-emphasise Eddie's femininity, and together with her rumbustious and unladylike behavior, they serve to neutralise any potential sexual tension between the coach and her players. Chawansky (2010) points to the "symbolic importance" of the locker room itself, which "provides a unique space within the realm of sport wherein myths and truths about gender and sexuality are both created and challenged" (p. 171). This normally exclusively homosocial space, where players are regularly in the nude and thus vulnerable, especially when considering the power imbalance between (clothed) coach and (naked) athlete, is disrupted by the female coach and the resulting potential for sexual tension this introduces.

In *Eddie*, a comical scene defuses this threat. When Eddie enters the locker room to discuss the game, she finds most of the players in the showers. At first, she continues her coaching monologue, but then suddenly interrupts herself as she becomes aware that the players in front of her are all naked and starts talking about the players' genitals amidst shrieks of laughter:

> What, they shrink up under water? I thought it was gonna be that much bigger, you know, you guys are like this [points to their height] and it's like this [indicates the size between her finger and thumb] it looks like a kind of pimple!

This scene, while somewhat hysterical, successfully de-eroticises the relationship between female coach and male athlete that the locker room might otherwise have provided. Later, when one player complains that coaches are never interested in the players as people and see them as dehumanised basketball machines, Eddie, like Coach McGrath before her, takes on a motherly role. Her caring and nurturing of the team by helping them with their personal problems, from marriage counseling to translating to career guidance, soon starts to improve the team's performance. Male coaches are occasionally afforded similar displays of care and kindness, such as when Coach Carter comforts one of his players after he appears at Carter's house in the middle of the night, having been part of a shoot out during a botched drug deal. However, the boundaries around such displays of affection and kindness are strictly policed, with respect, especially respect between men, receiving much more narrative attention than nurture.

Phyllis Saroka also takes on this motherly role for her team, and like Coach McGrath, she is similarly defended by her players. When a referee tells Coach Saroka to "shut up and sit down, godammit", reserve player Busy-bee (De'aundre Bonds) jumps at the referee: "Don't be talkin' like that to my coach, disrespectin' her!" The scene is less threatening than in *Wildcats*, as Busy-Bee is the least intimidating player of the team, with a slight frame and geeky glasses, but despite the underlying humor, it highlights the shift in the perception of the coach – she is now one of them and therefore deserves their protection. At the same time, she also protects them: when Spaceman (Terence Howard) is bullied by his science teacher Morris Bernstein (Scott Burkholder) to the point of desperation, Phyllis aggressively accosts Bernstein, and makes him apologise to Spaceman. She also visits Busy-bee in hospital after he has been shot in an attempted robbery, and helps Shorty when he is accused of trying to shoot someone. As she guides them through their personal crises, she develops a motherly fondness for her team, which eventually leads her to reject her restaurant dream and stay on as coach. Once desexualised and domesticated, it appears, the previously unruly femininity of the female coaches is once again under control and no longer threatens the hegemonic social order.

Conclusion

In Hollywood sports movies, male coaches almost never encounter the kind of resistance, hostility and aggression their female counterparts endure – authority and respect are quickly established and remain from then on unchallenged, as the examples from *Coach Carter* and *Remember the Titans* show. None of the three films discussed here, despite addressing the sexism that the gender of the coach brings out, manages to resolve this tension without resorting to the tired old trope of domesticating the phallic woman. It is both significant and disturbing that for the female coach, access to authority and power is dependent on permission granted by the men in the films. The films thus fail in their attempts to construct a feminist critique of male-dominated coaching practices in particular and sports as a male preserve in general.

While there have been increasing numbers of films with female athletes in the past 20 years, and growing critical interest in these, the same does not apply to films about female coaches, and in particular, films about female coaches of male athletes. The paucity of films featuring female coaches points beyond the sporting arena and reflects the more general sociocultural tensions regarding women and power. In cinema, these tensions are reflected in the excessive femininity of the "action babe" in films such as *Charlie's Angels* (McG, 2000) or the continuing demonisation of the career woman, such as the cold fashion editor Miranda Priestly in *The Devil Wears Prada* (David Frankel, 2006) and the foul-mouthed, self-absorbed, disgraced ex-CEO Michelle Darnell in *The Boss* (Ben Falcone, 2016). Beyond film, these tensions have come to prominence in the polarised presidential election cycle of 2016, where a political newcomer such as real-estate developer Donald Trump can accuse two-time senator and former Secretary of State Hillary Clinton of "playing the woman card" to get ahead in the elections. In this climate, it is unsurprising that there seem to be no further Hollywood films with female coaches on the horizon.

Perhaps the more recent, "glass-ceiling"-shattering hires of Becky Hammon, Jen Welter, Sarah Thomas and Kathryn Smith in the NFL and NBA will inspire a new generation of filmmakers to produce sports films in which female coaches are depicted as competent, authoritative and accepted as such by their teams regardless of gender. Or maybe we should simply celebrate the unruly femininity of Eddie Franklin, Molly McGrath and Phyllis Saroka, instead of trying to turn a (gender) blind eye.

Notes

1. Retrieved 22 December 2015.
2. *TheIndependent*http://www.independent.co.uk/sport/tennis/wimbledon-2014-andy-murray-and-am-lie-mauresmo-now-the-courtship-begins-9554396.html, "Andy Murray makes groundbreaking coaching hire with Amelie Mauresmo" *USA Today*, ftw.usatoday.com/2014/06/andy-murray-amelie-mauresmo-coach-woman, *The Express*, http://www.express.co.uk/sport/tennis/481288/Andy-Murray-gets-his-girl-guide-Amelie-Mauresmo-before-Wimbledon
3. Women coaching women is even more elusive, the only example since 1985 that I am aware of is the 2009 drama *The Mighty Macs*, which had only a limited release in the U.S.
4. While research on female athletes has increased manyfold, there has only been one attempt at investigating the depiction of female coaches in the chapter "Measured and Recorded: Cinematic Female Coaches" in Viridiana Lieberman's monograph *Sports Heroines on Film* (2015).
5. For a closer examination of abusive coaching practices as represented in Hollywood films, see Kerr et al. in this issue.
6. See also (Bonzel, 2013; Caudwell, 2009; Chare, 2015; Holmlund, 2002).
7. For a discussion of the figure of the phallic woman in film, see *The Monstrous Feminine* (Creed, 1993).
8. Humour has long been associated with the defusing of gender transgressions, see for example Chris Straayers' work on temporary transvestite narratives in mainstream comedies (Straayer, 2003).

Disclosure statement

No potential conflict of interest was reported by the author.

References

Acosta, R. V., & Carpenter, L. J. (2014). Women in intercollegiate sport. A longitudinal, national study, thirty seven year update, 1977–2014. Retrieved from http://www.acostacarpenter.org

Ashby, J. (2005). Postfeminism in the British frame. *Cinema Journal, 44*, 127–132.

Babington, B. (2014). *The sports film: Games people play*. New York, NY: Columbia University Press.

Baker, A. (2003). *Contesting identities: Sports in American film*. Urbana, IL: University of Illinois Press.

Bonzel, K. (2013). *A League of their Own*: The impossibility of the female sports hero. *Screening the Past, 37*, n.p.

Caudwell, J. (2009). *Girlfight* and *Bend it like Beckham*: Screening women, sport, and sexuality. *Journal of Lesbian Studies, 13*, 255–271.

Chare, N. (2015). *Sportswomen in cinema: Film and the frailty myth*. London: I.B.Tauris.

Chawansky, M. (2010). Put me in, Ms. Coach: Sexual rhetoric in the locker room. In L. K. Fuller (Ed.), *Sexual sports rhetoric: Historical and media contexts of violence* (pp. 169–177). New York, NY: Peter Lang.

Creed, B. (1993). *The monstrous-feminine: Film, feminism psychoanalysis*. London: Routledge.

Crosson, S. (2013). *Sport and film*. New York, NY: Routledge.

Gramsci, A. (1992). *Prison notebooks*. New York, NY: Columbia University Press.

Hargreaves, J. (2000). *Heroines of sport*. London: Routledge.

Holmlund, C. (2002). *Impossible bodies: Femininity and masculinity at the movies*. London: Routledge.

Hughey, M. W. (2014). *The white savior film: Content, critics, and consumption*. Philadelphia, PA: Temple University Press.

Lieberman, V. (2015). *Sports heroines on film: A critical study of cinematic women athletes, coaches and owners*. Jefferson, NC: McFarland.

Mosse, G. L. (1985). *Nationalism and sexuality: Respectability and abnormal sexuality in modern Europe*. New York, NY: H. Fertig.

Pollock, G. (1988). *Vision and difference: Femininity, feminism and the histories of Art*. London: Routledge.

Poulton, E., & Roderick, M. (2008). *Sport in films*. London: Routledge.

Rider, C. I., Wade, J., Swaminathan, A., & Schwab, A. (2016). Racial disparity in leadership: Performance-reward bias in promotions of national football league coaches. *Georgetown McDonough School of Business Research* (Paper No. 2710398). http://dx.doi.org/http://dx.doi.org/10.2139/ssrn.2710398

Sochen, J. (1993). The Prices of power: Women's depictions in film. In J. E. Combs (Ed.), *Movies and politics: The dynamic relationship* (pp. 97–113). New York, NY: Garland.

Straayer, C. (2003). Redressing the "Natural": The temporary transvestite film. In B. K. Grant (Ed.), *Film genre reader III* (pp. 417–442). Austin: University of Texas Press.

Tasker, Y. (1998). *Working girls*. London: Routledge.

Tudor, D. V. (1997). *Hollywood's vision of team sports: Heroes, race, and gender*. New York, NY: Garland.

Tuttle, L. (1988). *Heroines*. London: Harrap.

Filmography

Anspaugh, D., & De Haven, C. (1986). *Hoosiers*. United States: Orion Pictures.

Carter, T., & Gale, D. (2005). *Coach Carter*. United States: Paramount Pictures.

Chadha, G. (2002). *Bend it like Beckham*. United Kingdom: Rank Film Distribution.

REPRESENTATIONS OF SPORT COACHES IN FILM

Collector, R., & Chubb, C. (2006). *Believe in me*. United States: IFC Films.

Eastwood, C. (2004). *Million dollar baby*. United States: Warner Bros. Pictures.

Falcone, B. (2016). *The boss*. United States: Universal Pictures.

Frankel, D., & Finerman, W. (2006). *The devil wears prada*. United States: 20th Century Fox.

Gomer, S., & DeVito, D. (1996). *Sunset park*. United States: TriStar Pictures.

Levinson, B., & Crichton, M. (1994). *Disclosure*. United States: Warner Bros. Pictures.

Marshall, P., & Abbott, E. (1992). *A league of their own*. United States: Columbia Pictures.

McG & Goldberg, L. (2000). *Charlie's Angels*. United States: Columbia Pictures.

Nichols, M., & Wick, D. (1988). *Working girl*. United States: 20th Century Fox.

Rash, S., & Permut, D. (1996). *Eddie*. United States: Buena Vista Pictures/PolyGram Filmed Entertainment.

Ritchie, M., & Sylbert, A. (1986). *Wildcats*. United States: Warner Bros. Pictures.

Towne, R. (1982). *Personal best*. United States: Warner Bros. Pictures.

Yakin, B., & Bruckheimer, J. (2000). *Remember the titans*. United States: Buena Vista Pictures.

Sound coaching: tending to the heard in American football films

Nicholas Chare

Department of History of Art and Film Studies, Université de Montréal, Montréal, Canada

ABSTRACT
This study focuses on how the use of sound, particularly dialogue, in American football films contributes towards the depiction of varied forms of coaching behaviour and practice. Building on a pre-existing investigation that employed *Any Given Sunday* as a research tool to analyse motivational speeches, the study begins by addressing some of the difficulties that potentially accompany film-based research into sports coaching. It then examines how differing approaches to coaching involving emotional intelligence or the calculated use of performance data are communicated through dialogue such as motivational speeches. The study concludes by attending to the interrelated issues of sexism and zoomorphism in cinematic portrayals of emotion-driven football coaching.

"Do you hear me in there?" (Coach Bud Kilmer to his quarterback in *Varsity Blues*)

Introduction: sound check

This article focuses on relationships between coaching and sound as they feature in sports films about American football. There is a long-standing tradition of such films and a significant quantity and variety therefore exist. Drawing on the richness of this archive, specific examples will be subject to textual analysis as a means to highlight some of the ways in which a study of sound in relation to coaching in football films (and, by extension, in sports films more generally) can be enlightening. I will not be providing an overview of all extant American football films or engaging in sustained comparative analysis of films across historical periods or levels of play (high school, college, professional). My work is instead intended to serve as a general spur to more directed research on specific themes and issues as they appear in football films.

Sound in film registers in numerous ways, encompassing all the noises that can be heard (including the film score, if there is one) and also, usually, the spoken word or dialogue. A coach's dialogue can be self-directed (such as swearing to themselves) or addressed to players, assistants, the media, or spectators, among others. For Kracauer (1985), the inclusion of dialogue in a film increases its affinity to theatre (p. 128). Films with dialogue "convey plots in theatrical fashion" and "turn the spotlight on the actor, featuring him [sic] as an insoluble entity, and by the same token exile inanimate nature to the background" (Kracauer, 1985, p. 128). In this conception, the heard word lures the eye, drawing attention to speakers at the expense of their surrounds, emphasising figures over backdrop. Speech can, then, cause us to take our eye of the ball, to miss the bigger picture. Although dialogue forms the key aspect of the analyses that follow, efforts are therefore also sometimes made to hear beyond it, addressing other dimensions of the film soundtrack and its significance including its relationship to the image.

Generally, in sports films it is the pre-game or midgame motivational speech that assumes the greatest importance as dialogue. In recent research into the effectiveness of pregame speeches, Vargas-Tonsing and Guan (2007) refer to the mythology that surrounds such speeches which create "an expectation of heroic deeds and efforts of magnificent proportion" (p. 171). Vargas-Tonsing and Bartholomew (2006) discuss how pregame speeches have been captured in movies, specifically referencing "Win one for the Gipper" from *Knute Rockne: All American* (p. 918). The legendary quality of the motivational speech is both reflected in and reinforced by many other American football films that I will discuss. A number, such as *Any Given Sunday*, *Friday Night Lights* and *Remember the Titans*, feature seemingly game-changing talks to athletes. In *The Longest Yard*, when his prison guards are in danger of losing a tune-up game to a team of inmates, Warden Rudolph Hazen forcefully reminds his captain Wilhelm Knauer of the need to deliver an inspiring "pep talk". It is, however, a speech linked to ice hockey from the film *Miracle* that Vargas and Short (2011) reference at the beginning of an article on the perceptions that athletes have of pregame speeches. They quote from Kurt Russell's rendering of Herb Brook's motivational speech to the US ice hockey team prior to their first medal round game against the Soviet Union at the 1980 Winter Olympics (Vargas & Short, 2011, p. 28).

For Vargas and Short (2011), film enables famous speeches from sports history to "come alive" (p. 28). They add that "even though Hollywood may take some liberty when recreating these moments, sports psychology researchers have shown [...] that what coaches' say, when they say it, and how often they say it, can significantly alter the learning, development, and performance of athletes" (Vargas & Short, 2011, p. 28). Vargas and Short focus on films that depict actual events from sporting history but fictional films also often echo the motivational speeches of real-life coaches. Aaron Baker (2003), for example, draws attention to how the coach Tony D'Amato in *Any Given Sunday* gives talks in a style inspired by Vince Lombardi (p. 143). The film begins with an epigraph from Lombardi which is noteworthy "for its 'field of battle' imagery" (Babington, 2014, p. 101). There is therefore crossover between coaching and depictions of coaching in films. Real-life coaches influence filmic depictions of coaching. Films also seem to influence the expectations some athletes have of their coaches. Vargas and Short (2011), for instance, refer to an athlete who observes that although he likes his coach to keep pre-game speeches minimal there are "other guys 'who would love to see [the coach] deliver a speech straight out of *Miracle*'" (p. 29). This athlete signals how Hollywood depictions of coaching techniques potentially influence the expectations athletes have of their coaches in actual sporting situations.

I will begin by examining a study designed to investigate the motivational effectiveness of coach's pep talks which used the football film *Any Given Sunday* as a research tool. The study is revealing as much for the difficulties it raises in relation to using sports films to investigate coaching practices as for its actual findings. Building on this study, I will consider ways in which motivational speeches are employed in football films and assess what they reveal about the role of emotion in football coaching. I will go on to examine how some films depict coaches who do not display emotional intelligence relying instead on a calculated employment of performance data to engender competitive success. I will also analyse the impossibility of divorcing the acoustic from the visual in analyses of coaching in film. Finally I will examine what studying sound in relation to depictions of coaches in films reveals about the interrelated themes of gender and zoomorphism in American football.

Any given sound

Despite the clear relationship that exists between sports films and coaching, the significance of acoustic dimensions to sports films has seldom been examined for the practical insights they can provide into coaching. Gonzalez, Metzler, and Newton (2011), however, form a notable exception, using film clips as part of an exploratory study of the efficacy of inspirational speeches on collegiate football players. Their aim was to assess whether viewing a clip featuring a "pep talk" would inspire, motivate and influence the emotions of high-level college American football athletes. The researchers recognised that inspiration in sport is frequently characterised by "a powerful speech, quotation, or action clip from a film" (Gonzalez et al., 2011, p. 448). Popular perceptions of what inspires an athlete to success are often shaped by cinematic depictions. Given that the difficulties of measuring responses to speeches delivered in the field preclude sourcing data derived from actual game situations the researchers therefore felt film formed a viable alternative for investigating the impact of "pep talks" on inspiration, situational motivation and emotion in athletes.

The study involved two groups who watched different film clips. The two clips were both sourced from the canonical American football film *Any Given Sunday*. The inspirational clip which lasted 4 min 21 s comprised D'Amato's "Inches Speech", a half-time "pep talk" delivered when his team are in a losing situation. The other clip, a control which lasted 3 min 19 s, comprised "a montage of instructional-ly-focused clips" (Gonzalez et al., 2011, p. 450). Responses to the clips in relation to inspiration, situational motivation and emotional response were recorded. The research findings suggested that it was possible to inspire athletes with a film clip but raised inspiration did not necessarily generate increased motivation. The study, innovative and stimulating, nevertheless exhibits some shortcomings. These limitations highlight various difficulties that accompany using films featuring coaching for research purposes.

Some weaknesses of the study are openly recognised such as the vicarious nature of the experience of the athletes (Gonzalez et al., 2011, p. 449). The athletes are not being addressed directly but are watching other athletes being addressed. They must therefore "immerse themselves in a fictitious situation and imagine the actor was their coach" (Gonzalez et al., 2011, p. 449). The researchers admit that "it is possible that the actor's stage presence rather than the content of his speech was inspiring [or not] to the participant" (Gonzalez et al., 2011, p. 449). Stage presence refers to an actor's charisma, an elusive quality that commands an audi-ence's attention. There is an acknowledgement that Al Pacino, who plays the role of D'Amato, in acting as a coach may deliver speeches in a way that is qualitatively different to a real-life coach. Pacino supplements the content of the speech with "stage presence" whereas, it is implied, coaches simply deliver content. In reality, of course, there a numerous different modes of delivering content, coaches can be theatrical, some may be described as charismatic.

Gonzalez et al. (2011) also foreground that "any influence of the coach-athlete relationship cannot be accounted for in this particular study" (p. 449). The way a coach's speech is received is bound up with the often lengthy relationship she or he has had with an individual or group of athletes. A coach's speech which is out of character, such as an angry tirade, will likely impact an athlete more than a typical speech. The way a coach's speech is received within a film is also linked to what has happened prior to it in the narrative including how coach–athlete relationships have been portrayed up to that point. Cutting the "Inches Speech" out of the film and presenting it as a standalone monologue will impact upon the way it is interpreted. In *Any Given Sunday*, much of the significance of this speech derives from the audience's prior knowledge of D'Amato's alcohol problems, his loneliness, his precarious employment situation and his sometimes fraught past interactions with players and staff. By taking the "Inches Speech" out of its broader context, the researchers present athletes with "bleeding chunks" of *Any Given Sunday*. The expression "bleeding chunks" was first used by the critic Tovey (2015) to refer to the practice of plundering Wagner's operas for the "best bits" (such as the Ride of the Valkyries) on Wagner nights (pp. 254–255). For Tovey such a practice destroys the integrity of the overall work. It is clear from the research findings that the "Inches Speech" does not require knowledge of the rest of the film to have emotional impact and for its inspirational qualities to be recognised.

It is, however, unclear how the speech would have been received by the athletes in the context of the film as a whole.

Emotionally intelligent coaching

The inspirational effects of D'Amato's speech upon the athletes in Gonzalez, Metzler and Newton's experiment may be strongly linked to their being footballers. The coach spoke their language, not simply because the film was about American football but because the speech centred on emotion rather than planning. American Football as a sport potentially places distinct demands on coaches as it is a contact sport that is perceived as relying "heavily on arousal and less on information" (Vargas-Tonsing & Guan, 2007, p. 177). The plays used in football are scripted which may make players less interested in informational aspects in coaching contexts such as a pre-game speech. The American football coach invested in the power of a pre-game speech for influencing the outcome of games might therefore work to perfect skills of emotional choreography and place less emphasis on learning how to communicate strategy. Gonzalez et al. (2011) also recognise the specific emotional demands of American football and suggest the need for football athletes to be exalted and impassioned by a pep talk (p. 454). An intelligent American football coach will therefore likely tailor game day speeches to privilege the generation of specific emotions such as courage, hope, pride, togetherness, perhaps even anger.

In this context, coaches who fail to show emotion, those who are too cool and calculating, risk appearing out of touch in a contact sport such as football. Washington (2003) observes that football is exceptional because of the intense emotion it produces: "In the many sports I've played, I've never experienced anything like it ... the rush you get from all that contact, all that hitting, all that competition and maneuvering. It's the adrenaline" (p. 77). Football is about fright and the exhilaration of overcoming it. It is about fight over flight: finding courage in fear. It therefore requires a coach who is unafraid to feel. *Any Given Sunday* includes a character, the offensive co-ordinator Crozier, whose style of coaching is the inverse of this, whose observations to players are purely the result of crunching data. Crozier is regarded as a modern coach and D'Amato as an anachronism whose coaching, as Fuller (2010) foregrounds in her analysis of the film, is "old-style, constantly hollering" (p. 187). The conflict between the coaching styles of Crozier and D'Amato is introduced early in the film. Shortly before quarterback Willie Beaman is to be brought onto the field of play, D'Amato, who is pitch side, offers him some words of encouragement. Beaman is not wearing his helmet so he is unable to hear the tactical information Crozier is simultaneously seeking to relay to him via radio. Crozier, who is seated up in the gods, is therefore unable to get his message across while the grounded D'Amato can communicate what he feels is necessary to the player. Here a conflict over approaches to coaching is played out through who can and cannot be heard. D'Amato's more hands-on approach triumphs.

This theme forms one of many parallels between *Any Given Sunday* and *North Dallas Forty* (a loose adaptation of the book of the same name), an earlier film in which the coach B.A. Strother (lightly based on Tom Landry) and his assistants are also exponents of a data-driven coaching approach. The audience is introduced to Strother tapping at a computer keyboard. He tells his wide receiver Phil Elliott, "There's something that runs through all this data Phil. It's immaturity. Your immaturity. You lack seriousness". It subsequently becomes clear that this "immaturity" is linked to a refusal to slavishly follow instructions. Strother's coaching philosophy is most clearly expressed in a lengthy scene in which the team study silent video footage of a recent game. The video is being used as a coaching tool. Strother invites the players to view and comment on their performance. One athlete, Stallings, is berated for his indecision. Strother asserts that "There's no room in this business for uncertainty. *No room!*" He then asks Elliott to describe a play. Elliot's response, "Well [pause] we scored a touchdown", elicits considerable mirth. Strother, however, is not amused and begins a lengthy diatribe, involving much finger-pointing, which encompasses his coaching philosophy:

> Oh you think it's funny [shouting]! Well I fail to see any humour at all. Maxwell changed the play I sent in. Elliott broke his pattern. And the catch was a fluke. There's no room for flukes in winning game plans. Why do you think we go over and over the print outs of the game plans? Because deviating from that plan can cost us the championship. Now if there are some of you who are not interested in being champions, why then you laugh, relax, have a good time but you'll do it on somebody else's football team. Not mine. [Pause]. The key to being a good professional is consistency and the computer measures that quality. No one of you is as good as that computer. I hope I am understood.

This rigid conception of coaching seemingly leaves little scope for emotion, nor for spontaneity or improvisation, given that the computer is the yardstick against which the players are judged. The "fluke", the event that is not scripted in advance, the lucky break, the product of chance, is anathema. Coaching is all about controlling outcomes, about control. In one scene, as if to reinforce his disciplinarian credentials, Strother is shown watching a practice session from a viewing platform that resembles a guard tower, his megaphone in hand, at the ready to assert acoustic control when necessary (often it is the coach's whistle which provides sound discipline).

Strother is also given to bombarding his players with statistics linked to previous games: "Pass completions were 49%. 6.3% less than reasonable. And it's 19% less than our outstanding". For some of the players the reliance on data analysis is associated with the commodification of football, a symptom of it. After losing the final game of the season, one of the front four, Shaddock, responds to criticism from the assistant coach, Johnson, by stating "Well shit, you never give us anything to bring in the game except your fucking facts and tendencies. To you it's just a business but to us it's still got to be a sport!" Rigauer's (1981) Marxist analysis of modern sport discusses how, in top-level sport, auditing performance has become crucial and "numbers – with all the weight of their technical-rational symbolism – have assumed a central significance" (pp. 56–57). The facts Shaddock refers to, measurements, percentages, are designed to aid increased productivity, to enable more wins. Coaching as an exercise in quantitative analysis and the politics it embodies is, however, rejected by him. The coaching-staff are berated for not displaying emotion, for being too calculating and dispassionate.

The reality of the portrayal of coaching in *North Dallas Forty* is actually more complex than Shaddock's perception of it. Strother understands the need to harness emotions. He is a master manipulator of feelings. In this context, Elliott's facial expression after a fight engineered by Strother between two defensive players in a practice session suggests that he recognises the coach's psychological prowess. Strother may slyly solicit emotional responses from the team but ultimately he and his staff are condemned for failing to inspire. Inspiration, for Shaddock, would be *showing* passion. Strother is capable of angry outbursts when his data-driven instructions are not implemented but is otherwise too controlled. The only time he comes close to a more complex emotional response to football is when the team loses its final game due to a fumbled catch. There is a shot of Strother struggling to control his emotion. It is accompanied by the voice of a commentator describing the loss of the game combined with downbeat and unsettling minimalist non-diegetic music. The audience watches his tense features contort until he finally exhales and regains a measure of composure. The subdued music here provides psychological insight, figuring Strother's upset. He strives not to show his emotions but the music reveals them, the audience shares in them. D'Amato, by contrast, wears his emotions on his sleeve, exulting in their display.

Audio-visual coaching

The shot of Strother striving to suppress his distress (an emotion culturally coded as unmanly) derives its impact as much from what the audience hears (the commentary and the music) as from what they see. As Prendergast (1992) observes, however, images often also influence the way we hear things in films (p. 217). The relationship between the audible and the visible is symbiotic. The study produced by Gonzalez et al. (2011) is again revealing in this context. They discover that the instructionally focussed montage (the precise details of which are not provided) which they screen for one group of athletes fails to inspire. The reference to this footage as a montage demonstrates their knowledge of cinematic technique. Montage is the product of editing and usually comprises a speedy succession of different camera shots. The potential role of camerawork and editing in the emotional and motivational impact, or lack thereof, of the "Inches Speech" and the technique-oriented scenes included in the control clip is not examined beyond a brief reference to this clip containing "very cinematically strong visual images" (Gonzalez et al., 2011, p. 454).

Kracauer's (1985) observations about dialogue and theatre discussed earlier foreground the impossibility of divorcing the audible from the visible. Any consideration of film sound in a given scene, for example, must also take into account the imagery, or absence thereof, that accompanies it. In the "Inches Speech", it is clear that choices of shot potentially provide emotional cues to viewers as they show the emotional reactions of the onscreen athletes, their visible utterances, their nods of assent. The athletes participating in the study see others seemingly being inspired and potentially mirror that response. It might therefore have been preferable to play only the audio of the pep talk and of the instructional sequences to the groups. In reality, however, a coach's speech will always also include visual information. She or he will look at players, gesticulate, perhaps frown or smile. Their facial expressions, gestures and general appearance will also influence how what they say is received. Sound, as Michel Chion (1994) notes, frames the film image, influencing its reception (p. 7). The image also informs how sound including speech is understood. The same can be said of everyday life. Any speech, including a motivational speech, is always delivered accompanied by non-verbal cues and other visual material.

In this context, the film *Wildcats* is informative. In a pep-talk delivered the night before the first game of a new season, Coach Molly McGrath uses a combination of verbal cues and visual symbolism to make her point that the failings of this team the season before have no contemporary relevance:

> This is last year's schedule. [Sets light to the schedule]. It's gone. Forget it. You guys are better now. *Much better.* Now tomorrow's our first game. *Forget* the past. *Concentrate* on tomorrow and don't be nervous tonight.

McGrath stresses particular words, emphasises their importance, reinforcing the improved ability of the team, the need to be focussed and the necessity of forgetting past inadequacies. This last point is made more powerfully through the striking image of the burning of the old schedule. A remnant of the past, a reminder of it, is literally consigned to oblivion in order to serve as a powerful visual metaphor for what the athletes need to do. Simply hearing McGrath's speech, without the accompanying imagery, would likely considerably reduce its impact.

It is possible to envisage showmanship of the kind employed by McGrath being used in a real world situation. Sometimes, however, the visuals in film depictions of coaches are intrinsic to the medium. A good example occurs towards the end of *Varsity Blues*, when the dictatorial head coach Bud Kilmer loses the faith of his players during half-time in a crucial game. After physically assaulting his quarterback, Jonathon "Mox" Moxon, Kilmer exits the locker room shouting "Let's go, let's go, let's go!" and clapping his hands repeatedly, hoping to inspire his hitherto subservient team to follow him. None of the players respond and Kilmer ends up alone in a corridor. His final words of encouragement are directed at no one, heard only by himself and the audience viewing the film. The coach's banishment, his rejection by the team, is reinforced by how the scene is shot. The corridor is filmed with minimal lighting using a blue-filter. It is cold, tenebrous. The way this space is shot serves to highlight Kilmer's isolation. It is crafted to act as visual metaphor. The film score, at this moment subdued, reflective, complements and supplements the seen, reinforcing Kilmer's silhouetted solitude. Audio and visual together voice a powerful rejection of a particular approach to coaching, one in which the long term physical and psychological welfare of players is unimportant.

For Kilmer, players are reduced to mere appendages of flesh in gridiron, simply the means to further his competitive ends. This view of the athletes is prefigured in much earlier films such as *Trouble along the Way*, in which the coach Steve Williams describes a group of freshmen who will form his football team as "a nice looking mountain of flesh". The young men are viewed by Wilson foremost as bodies, appreciated for their bulk, muscle, sinew, with their minds unimportant. It is powerful bodies that coaches frequently view as of central importance. In *Varsity Blues*, the team develop a collective consciousness that rebels against Kilmer's objectification of them, his reduction of them to unthinking instruments for his success. The team will ultimately triumph without Kilmer at the helm. It is, of course, possible to interpret the team's victory as still due to Kilmer, to his reaching into the shadowlands of the personalities of his athletes over the course of a season, drawing unacknowledged dimensions of their strength and determination from out of their frailties and fears. Some coaches continue to believe that what most would regard as emotionally abusive behaviours of the kind practiced by Kilmer, regularly intimidating and shouting at players, form legitimate ways to develop mental toughness in athletes (Owusu-Sekyere & Gervis, 2014). There is also still a marked tendency in sports films to link sporting achievement with "tough love" approaches to coaching of the kind embodied by Kilmer.

Manning up

In *Varsity Blues*, Kilmer abuses the masculinity of his players to foster the toughness he believes is essential for football, rounding on Moxon at one point shouting "Your daddy was a no talent pussy but at least he listened". Pussy is a slang term for the vagina. In his use of gendered language, the coach therefore seemingly links being female with lacking sporting prowess. The kind of language used in *Varsity Blues* is commonplace in American football films and reflects long-standing attitudes about manliness that are bound up with the game and exploited by coaches. Lieberman (2015) has identified the football field as an enduring "realm of hegemonic masculinity" and "a mainstay producing patriarchal ideas opposing gender equity" (p. 135) and Dundes (1978) has explored how insults in American football are frequently linked to behaviour labelled as feminine with curse words such as pussy, cunt and sissy commonplace (p. 85). Coaches in football films often refer to their players as feminine to rile and thereby motivate them. Player-coach

Wilhelm Knauer chews out his team in *The Longest Yard* by suggesting "you're playing like a bunch of girls – candy asses". In *Wildcats*, comparable language is used by one of the players, slot receiver Krushinski, to describe what he perceives to be a subpar performance. At half time in the final game of the season, which the Wildcats are losing, Krushinski observes: "they're champions and we are a bunch of dildos!" Here, as Chawansky (2010) notes in her analysis of *Wildcats*, Krushinski suggests his team are masquerading as men, their phallic credentials rendered questionable, faked (p. 175).

Coaching practices that exploit the discourse of masculinity are centred upon the warrior ethos of American football. Kilmer in *Varsity Blues* addresses Billy Bob, an offensive guard who may be suffering from concussion, as his "soldier". In the point of view shot from Bob's perspective, Kilmer's face fills the frame as he says this. The commanding officer is shown to be invading the personal space of his grunt. In *Remember the Titans*, Coach Herman Boone takes his athletes to the site of the battle of Gettysburg as a means to encourage them to address the racism that divides them. In asking them to choose whether they are on the same side or not, the visit invites the athletes to view themselves as soldiers. Boone also behaves towards his athletes like a drill instructor. His vision of himself, however, is as a dictator: "This is no democracy. It is a dictatorship. I am the law". Here, coaching is framed in strictly top down terms with no room for shared leadership of the kind espoused, for example, by Jones and Standage (2006). In *Varsity Blues*, Kilmer is also presented as dictatorial. When he is speaking at a high school pep rally prior to a game against rivals Banville, Kilmer quiets the exuberant crowd with a gesture reminiscent of a Nazi salute, the *Hitlergruß*. Here, his high-handedness as a coach is signalled through a visible utterance, one which also demonstrates his power through his ability to control the acoustic.

The coach as strongman is a staple of football films, the coach as strongwoman a rarity. This renders *Wildcats*, featuring a woman coach of a boy's high school team, particularly interesting. *Wildcats* pulls no punches in terms of its depiction of the sexism that pervades football. On her first encounter with the Central High School football team she will coach, McGrath is subject to sexually abusive comments. One player observes "I like your tits" and another loudly opines "Coach has this really cute ass – you notice that". She is fragmented into bodily parts, verbally reduced to "tits and ass", sexually fetishised and objectified. McGrath is ultimately forced to prove herself as worthy of coaching the team, as being more than mere "eye candy". She demonstrates her eminence via an endurance test.[1] This test involves the whole team running for as far and as long as they each can until only one of them is left standing. If McGrath is not the "last man standing", if she cannot attest to her female masculinity, she vows to quit.[2] Lieberman (2015) observes that this test takes McGrath "out of the coaching role, placing her side by side with her players" (p. 139). It can also be viewed as a coaching approach that involves leading by example. In this, McGrath's actions are not dissimilar to those of Coach Wilson in *Trouble along the Way* who physically demonstrates what he expects his players to do, showing them how to position and to move their bodies.

In addition to proving McGrath's physical stamina, the test also shows her to be cerebral, demonstrating her notable understanding of sporting psychology, her ability to "psych out" the competition. When only the coach and a player called Trumaine are left running, McGrath says: "I forgot to tell you, I ran the Boston marathon". Trumaine responds "Oh shit!" McGrath then adds "Twice!" doubling the impact of what may or may not be a true statement. Trumaine gives up shortly afterwards. Utterances of this kind provide an example of Machiavellian tactics (Paulhus, Molin, & Schuchts, 1979). Unnerving or psyching-out opponents can provide substantial competitive advantage. The run is performed to the non-diegetic accompaniment of Mavis Staples's song "Show me how it works". McGrath *shows* that what works for a male coach in relation to a team of male athletes may not work for a female coach. She is forced to earn the respect of her players through physically out-performing them. She also audibly *shows* the audience that competitive success can involve guile as much as stamina. She is a smart coach as well as a fit one. This positive representation of a female football coach is important given the numerous barriers actual female coaches perceive to exist in their profession, including low perceived confidence and competence (LaVoi & Dutove, 2012). There is a need for female coaches as role models who can positively influence the development of self-esteem in women (Graham, McKenna, & Fleming, 2013). In this context, McGrath's assertive acoustic comportment can potentially audibly contribute to shifting perceptions about women's coaching capacities.[3]

Catcalls of the wild

The gendered rhetoric that characterises football films, including its denigration of women, is frequently bound up with the zoomorphism that features in dialogue. Links between football and the animal kingdom have already been made in research on the game. Dundes's (1978) psychoanalytically informed reading of football draws on examples from the natural world to explain the three point stance, "bending over in a distinct stooped position" is comparable to non-human primates engaging in "presenting" (p. 81). Dundes explains:

> Presenting refers to a subordinate animal's turning its rump towards a higher ranking or dominant one. The center thus presents to the quarterback – just as linesmen do to the backs in general (p. 81).

Here the players engage in becoming nonhuman animals, assuming positions that signal the dominance of the quarterback, their status as "top dog", the alpha male. In this context, films such as *Quarterback Princess* in which the male centre, "aping" nonhuman primates, "presents" to a female athlete, the quarterback Tami Maida, or *Necessary Roughness* where the male quarterback kneels to hold the ball for a female kicker, Lucy Draper, possess a queer potential. The films present dynamics that deviate from the norms which usually regulate gender in football.

The football field, conventionally gendered as a masculine space and involving displays of dominance between biologically male athletes, becomes a site where athletic ability cuts across existing gendered and sexed identities. The coach, however, is absent from Dundes's analysis and excluded from the emancipatory dimensions to *Necessary Roughness* and *Quarterback Princess*.

Coaches in football films usually serve to frame others as nonhuman animals from the sidelines, keeping their distance from the "bestiary" that is the field. The animal names ascribed to the fictional teams in many of the films under consideration here, the Ampipe Bulldogs (*All the Right Moves*), the Cougars (*Trouble Along the Way*), the Coyotes (*Varsity Blues*), the Permian High School Panthers (*Friday Night Lights*), the Miami Sharks (*Any Given Sunday*), the Manassas Tigers (*Undefeated*), the Fighting Timberwolves (*The Program*), the Wildcats (*The Wildcats*), certainly encourage the athletes to think of themselves as a pack of animals. The names of teams often also inform how coaches address their players. In *Wildcats*, for instance, living- or not living-up to the team name is a recurring theme. After McGrath bests her players in the test of stamina, she calls them all pussies. As discussed earlier, pussy is a term of abuse used to denigrate male players and call into question their masculinity. As slang for the female genitalia and, by extension, for being female, the slight is associated with being cowardly and weak. In *Wildcats*, however, "pussy" functions as a double-entendre. It also refers to "pussy cat". Wildcats are not pussy cats, domestic felines. To call the players pussies is also to accuse them of not living up to their team name.

This connection is made clear later when the Wildcats are due to play the Cougars. In her halftime pep talk, McGrath asserts that the "Cougars will be nothing but a furball when we're done with them!" Furballs are hairballs that can accumulate in the digestive tracts of nonhuman animals such as cats but furball is also a term of endearment for a kitten. McGrath therefore humorously questions the mountain lion credentials of the Cougars, figuring them as kittens, as cute and cuddly. The expression "sex kitten" can also be used to describe a young, sexually appealing woman.[4] Suitably inspired by McGrath's kittenish words, Trumaine shouts "Yeah! Let's go eat some pussy!" Eating pussy, of course, means performing cunnilingus and effeminizes the Cougars. Here, however, it also figures them as domesticated, as soft, compared to the Wildcats, the real big cats. In *Wildcats*, links between femininity and animality are foregrounded through word-play. There is a long tradition in Western culture of linking women with nonhuman animals (to the detriment of both) (see, for instance, Gruen, 1993). This is reflected in *Wildcats*. In *The Freshman*, the surname of the central character, inept footballer Harold Lamb, does comparable work, signalling his meekness, his masculine lack, albeit not by directly referencing femininity.[5]

In *All the Right Moves* the team's name also influences the coach's behaviour. In training, Coach Nickerson manhandles one of his players, telling him "You're a dog. Get down on your knees and growl." The player obeys. His non-verbal, "bestial" vocalisations are meant to prove that he can live up to being a Bulldog. He is encouraged to take pride in animality. This does not signal a positive bringing into question of traditional structures of domination in Western cultural human–nonhuman animal relations. From *All the Right Moves* it is clear that to be a bulldog is to embrace hostility. Slovenko (1994) has observed in the context of basketball that the nonhuman animals used in team names are associated with "vicious or aggressive tendencies" (pp. 585–86). Nuessel (1994) similarly suggests perceived "vicious or predatory tendencies" inform the choice of nonhuman animal inspired athletics team nicknames such as bulldogs and wildcats (p. 101). Being a nonhuman animal in football is to cast off all traces of being civilised, to revel in violent impulses. In his ethnographic study of a high school football season at a South Texas town, Foley (1990) explains that "players who consistently inflicted outstanding hits were called animals, studs, bulls, horses or gorillas" (p. 127). The animal metaphors used in films therefore seem to reflect the real-life language of football. These metaphors are like most nonhuman animal metaphors in that they "perpetuate a contemptuous view of nonhuman beings that fosters their oppression" (Dunayer, 2001, p. 157).

A scene in *Necessary Roughness* ably captures the conception of animality that informs most film portrayals of football. At half time during the final college game of the season, the temporary head coach of the Texas State University Fighting Armadillos, Wally Riggendorf, endeavours to inspire his team who are losing badly. He forcefully suggests that they emulate the way their usual head coach, Ed Gennero, behaved as a player: "He played like a goddam wildman. No, like a goddam rampaging beast". As Riggendorf delivers this speech, he tears of the suit jacket he has been wearing. This fashion statement forms at once a rejection of the suit's white-collar connotations, for Riggendorf coaching is akin to manual labour, and a demonstration of the kind of wildness he is calling for. He moults, shedding the semblance of civility the suit provides, embracing his "brutishness". The team respond to Riggendorf's clarion call by finding their inner "beast", ultimately winning the game.

The "animal" status of the players also manifests in their subservience to the coach. *Necessary Roughness* is again revealing in this context. At one point the quarterback, Paul Blake, confides to his lover, Suzanne Carter, that he cannot discuss his feelings with his coach: "I can't talk to him. I'm a football player. He can't talk to me like I was human". In Blake's eyes, it appears that the bestial rhetoric employed by coaches towards their players is dehumanising. Coaches do not regard the players as equals but as lesser beings, as "animals". The language used by coaches and owners in the films reinforces the idea of football players as "brutes". Warden Rudolph Hazen in *The Longest Yard* describes the team which he manages as "overpriced beef". In a television interview watched by Coach Boone in *Remember the Titans*, a rival coach calls two of his players "prize bulls". The players are here referred to as beef cattle or show stock. Blake's remarks to Carter, however, suggest the players are usually viewed as workhorses, draught animals who must unthinkingly labour for their masters. Although coaches in

American football films may occasionally act brutally towards their athletes it is rare that a coach is portrayed as a "brute". An exception may be Coach Boone in *Remember the Titans* whose depiction Gregory Cranmer and Tina Harris suggest is influenced by the racial stereotype of the buck or brute. Cranmer and Harris (2015) argue that a sexually charged exchange between the coach and a player called Bertier in which Boone affirms he is the "daddy" plays on fears of the hypersexualised black male, the rutting stag (p. 163).

In football films, the animality of the players is seemingly confirmed through those moments of extreme exertion where they are reduced to grunting and gasping, screaming and moaning. In his essay "Listening", Barthes (2002) compared the infant's acquisition of language to a game of catch, suggesting that "Listening is that game of catch [*jeu d'attrape*] of signifiers by which the *infans* becomes a speaking being" (p. 348).[6] The verb *attraper* can be used to refer to catching a physical object (such as a football) and also to catching a snatch of conversation. In football, a game that prizes good catching, the players go in reverse, speech often giving way, in a kind of acoustic fumble, to non-verbal vocalisations. Their regression to non-speaking beings, "grunts", ostensibly affirms their becoming "animal". The coach, however, despite screaming and shouting, never loses their verbal composure. They are the voice of humanity.

Landsberg (2010) has examined how dialogue often has a distancing effect on film audiences whereas other human sounds prompt a visceral, bodily response that fosters intimacy (p. 20).[7] In this context, the coach's vocal self-possession discourages our identifying with them whereas we are animated by the non-verbal vocalisations of the athletes, our bodies identifying with their pain and exertion, feeling it. In real games, the sounds of the players as they labour on the field are largely inaudible to spectators. It is only in football films that these sounds are amplified, made to mean. Their significance is clearly negative. It signals their and our becoming "animal" with animality seemingly in part equated with embracing "raw emotion". The coach disquietingly facilitates heightened state of emotion through recourse to a zoomorphism which often intersects with racism and sexism.

Conclusion: the sound and the fury

This study of sound in football films shows that many of the lived realities of football coaching are reflected and reinforced in cinematic depictions of the sport. These range from practical matters like the need to privilege emotional input at specific moments in coaching (such as during the delivery of a motivational speech) to broader issues including the pervasive sexism that still characterises gridiron. Sexism as it is articulated in the films is often bound up with negative metaphors that are linked to nonhuman animals. Players are often feminised and/ or figured as "beasts" by onscreen coaches as they strive to arouse emotion in their players. As with real life football coaching, fostering appropriate emotional responses is seen as crucial to ensuring on-field success. The coaches in the films though often engage in degrading behaviours towards their athletes in order to generate such responses. In spite of this, some films also demonstrate how cinema as an art form can additionally provide powerful critiques of negative football coaching practices involving physical and verbal abuse. American football films, full of sound and fury, therefore signify much of interest and repay careful listening.

Notes

1. The difficulty of real-life female coaches establishing credibility with male athletes is well documented (see, for example, LaFountaine & Kamphoff, 2016).
2. The coach in American football is still a masculine-coded figure so McGrath can be seen to embody a form of female masculinity as Halberstam (1998) conceives of it. Female masculinity encompasses the extension of activities and traits culturally coded as masculine to women. For Halberstam, "a major step toward gender parity [...] is the cultivation of female masculinity" (p. 272).
3. For a detailed analysis of how the field of sound forms a site of struggle for gender equality in sport see my chapter on boxing films in *Sportswomen in Cinema* (Chare, 2015, pp. 41–66).
4. See, for example, the film *Kitten with a Whip* starring Ann-Margret as Jody Dvorak, the titular "kitten" with a whip, as a seductive female delinquent.
5. The character of Harold Lamb is played by Harold Lloyd. Lloyd made an earlier film called *The Lamb* which the surname also makes reference to. Crosson (2013) provides an insightful reading of how the character of Lamb in *The Freshman* enables Lloyd to critique football as a hypermasculine sport (pp. 44–46).
6. My translation.
7. See also the discussion of comparable acoustic phenomenon in my essay "Sound Policing" (Chare, 2012).

Acknowledgements

Thanks to Katharine Bonzel and the two anonymous reviewers for their insightful comments on earlier drafts of this paper.

Disclosure statement

No potential conflict of interest was reported by the author.

References

Babington, B. (2014). *The sports film: Games people play*. London: Wallflower.
Baker, A. (2003). *Contesting identities: Sports in American film*. Urbana: University of Illinois Press.
Barthes, R. (2002). Ecoute [1977]. In R. Barthes (Ed.), *Oeuvres complètes V* (pp. 340–352). Paris: Éditions de Seuil.

Chare, N. (2012). Sound policing: Attending to acoustic matters in *The Shield*. In N. Ray (Ed.), *Interrogating The Shield* (pp. 43–64). Syracuse: Syracuse University Press.

Chare, N. (2015). *Sportswomen in cinema: Film and the frailty myth*. London: IB Tauris.

Chawansky, M. (2010). Put me in, Ms. Coach: Sexual rhetoric in the locker room. In L. K. Fuller (Ed.), *Sexual sports rhetoric: Historical and media contexts of violence* pp. 169–177). New York,NY: Peter Lang.

Chion, M. (1994). *Audio-vision: Sound on screen*. New York, NY: Columbia University Press.

Cranmer, G. A., & Harris, T. M. (2015). "White-side, strong-side": A critical examination of race and leadership in *Remember the Titans*. *Howard Journal of Communications, 26*, 153–171.

Crosson, S. (2013). *Sport and film*. London: Routledge.

Dunayer, J. (2001). *Animal equality: Language and liberation*. Derwood: Ryce Publishing.

Dundes, A. (1978). Into the endzone for a touchdown: A psychoanalytic consideration of American football. *Western Folklore, 37*, 75–88.

Foley, D. E. (1990). The great American football ritual: Reproducing race, class, and gender inequality. *Sociology of Sport Journal, 7*, 111–135.

Fuller, L. K. (2010). Foul language: A feminist perspective on (American) football rhetoric. In L. K. Fuller (Ed.), *Sexual sports rhetoric: Historical and media contexts of violence* (pp. 179–192). New York, NY: Peter Lang.

Gonzalez, S. P., Metzler, J. N., & Newton, M. (2011). The influence of a simulated 'pep talk' on athlete inspiration, situational motivation, and emotion. *International Journal of Sports Science and Coaching, 6*, 445–459.

Graham, L., McKenna, M., & Fleming, S. (2013). "What d'you know, you're a girl!" Gendered experiences of sport coach education. *Journal of Hospitality, Leisure, Sport and Tourism Education, 13*, 70–77.

Gruen, L. (1993). Dismantling oppression: An analysis of the connection between women and animals. In G. Gaard (Ed.), *Ecofeminism: Women, animals, nature* (pp. 60–90). Philadelphia, PA: Temple University Press.

Halberstam, J. (1998). *Female masculinity*. Durham: Duke University Press.

Jones, R., & Standage, M. (2006). First among equals: Shared leadership in the coaching context. In R. L. Jones (Ed.), *The sports coach as educator: Reconceptualising sports coaching* (pp. 65–76). Abingdon: Routledge.

Kracauer, S. (1985). Dialogue and sound. In E. Weis & J. Bolton (Eds.), *Film sound: Theory and practice* (pp. 126–142). New York, NY: Columbia University Press.

LaFountaine, J., & Kamphoff, C. S. (2016). Coaching boys' high school teams: Female coaches' experiences and perceptions. *International journal of Sports Science & Coaching, 11*, 27–38.

Landsberg, A. (2010). Waking the *Deadwood* of history: Listening, language, and the 'aural visceral'. *Rethinking History, 14*, 531–549.

LaVoi, N. M., & Dutove, J. K. (2012). Barriers and supports for female coaches: An ecological model. *Sports Coaching Review, 1*, 17–37.

Lieberman, V. (2015). *Sports heroines on film: A critical study of cinematic women athletes, coaches and owners*. Jefferson, NC: McFarland.

Nuessel, F. (1994). Objectionable sport team designations. *Names, 42*, 101–119.

Owusu-Sekyere, F., & Gervis, M. (2014). Is creating mentally tough players a masquerade for emotional abuse? In D. Rhind & C. Brackenridge (Eds.), *Researching and enhancing athlete welfare* (pp. 44–48). Brunel: Brunel University Press.

Paulhus, D., Molin, J., & Schuchts, R. (1979). Control profiles of football players, tennis players, and nonathletes. *The Journal of Social Psychology, 108*, 199–205.

Prendergast, R. M. (1992). *Film music: A neglected art* (2nd ed.). New York, NY: Norton.

Rigauer, B. (1981). *Sport and work*. New York, NY: Columbia University Press.

Slovenko, R. (1994). Politically correct team names. *The Journal of Psychiatry and Law, 22,* 585–592.

Tovey, D. F. (2015). *Symphonies and other orchestral works.* New York, NY: Dover.

Vargas, T. M., & Short, S. E. (2011). Athletes' perceptions of the psychological, emotional, and performance effects of coaches' pre-game speeches. *International Journal of Coaching Science, 5,* 27–43.

Vargas-Tonsing, T. M., & Bartholomew, J. B. (2006). An exploratory study of the effects of pregame speeches on team efficacy beliefs. *Journal of Applied Social Psychology, 36,* 918–933.

Vargas-Tonsing, T. M., & Guan, J. (2007). Athletes' preferences for informational and emotional pre-game speech content. *International Journal of Sports Science and Coaching, 2,* 171–180.

Washington, L. (2003). The varsity coach smiled. In J. Gottesman (Ed.), *Game face: What does a female athlete look like?* (pp. 76–77). New York, NY: Random House.

Filmography

Bruckheimer, J., & Yakin, B. (2000). *Remember the Titans.* USA: Buena Vista.

Buckner, R., & Bacon, L. (1940). *Knute Rockne: All American.* USA: Warner Bros.

Ciardi, M., & O'Connor, G. (2004). *Miracle.* USA: Buena Vista.

Deutsch, S., & Chapman, M. (1983) *All the right moves.* USA: 20th Century Fox.

Donner, R., & Stone, O. (1999). *Any given sunday.* USA: Warner Bros.

Goodman, G., & Black, N. (1983). *Quarterback princess.* USA: CBS.

Grazer, B., & Berg, P. (2004). *Friday night lights.* USA: Universal.

Keller, H., & Heyes, D. (1964). *Kitten with a whip.* USA: Universal.

Lloyd, H., Newmeyer, F., & Taylor, S. (1925). *The freshman.* USA: Pathé.

Neufeld, M., & Dragoti, S. (1991). *Necessary roughness.* USA: Paramount.

Yablans, F., & Kotcheff, T. (1979). *North Dallas 40.* USA: Paramount.

Roach, H., Lloyd, H., & Pratt, G. (1918). *The lamb.* USA: Pathé.

Rothman, T., & Ward, D. S. (1993). *The program.* USA: Buena Vista.

Ruddy, A. S., & Aldrich, R. (1974). *The longest yard.* USA: Paramount.

Shavelson, M., & Curtiz, M. (1953). *Trouble along the way.* USA: Warner Bros.

Martin, T. J., & Zipper, G. (2011). *Undefeated.* USA: Zipper Bros.

Sylbert, A., & Ritchie, M. (1986). *Wildcats.* USA: Warner Bros.

Tollin, M., & Robbins, B. (1999). *Varsity blues.* USA: Paramount.

Film depictions of emotionally abusive coach–athlete interactions

Gretchen Kerr, Ashley Stirling and Ahad Bandealy

Faculty of Kinesiology and Physical Education, University of Toronto, Toronto, Canada

ABSTRACT
This study examined film portrayals of coach–athlete interactions in 19 popular, North American, sport films, with a focus on emotional abuse within the coach–athlete relationship. Using a confirmatory thematic approach, themes within the films were coded deductively relative to pre-determined categories derived from previous literature on athletes' experiences of emotional abuse in sport. In total, 346 emotionally abusive interactions were observed. Emotionally abusive coaching practices were most frequently used by head coaches in the forms of verbal comments, physically threatening behaviours, and the denial of attention and support against athletes. The majority of the incidents occurred in athletic venues in response to sport-related performance errors and in the presence of bystanders. Recommendations are made to empirically explore the potential of film portrayals to contribute to the normalisation of emotionally abusive coaching practices.

Introduction

Concerns about harmful sport coaching practices have been expressed in both public and scholarly domains for some time. In the 1970s, scholarly attention on harmful coaching practices was seen through such contributions as Orlick and Boterill's book *Every Kid Can Win* (1975) in which the authors addressed the potential loss of childhood as a result of coaches' emphases on winning outcomes. In Joan Ryan's 2005 popular, non-fiction book, *Little Girls in Pretty Boxes*, she wrote about various harmful coaching practices experienced by young female gymnasts and skaters, including excessive physical training, pressures to remain thin, and a singular focus on sport to the exclusion of other developmentally-appropriate endeavours. Similar concerns were addressed at that time in scholarly publications such as the *New England Journal of Medicine* (1996) in which Tofler and colleagues criticised the restricted identity, injuries, and the potential for physical and psychological abuse of young athletes. More recently, a specific focus on emotionally abusive coaching practices within the theoretical framework of child maltreatment has arisen.

Emotional abuse is characterised by patterns of non-physical harmful interactions within a relationship between a child and caregiver (Glaser, 2002). The nature of the relationship between the child and caregiver is a key element of this definition; it must be a critical one as defined by the child's dependence upon the adult for a sense of security, trust and fulfilment of needs (Crooks & Wolfe, 2007). Although a critical relationship was first used to describe the parent–child relationship, research has since extended critical relationships to include other adults such as teachers, babysitters and coaches, who are often responsible for the care of children (Wachtel, 1999). Furthermore, a pattern of emotionally harmful behaviours within a critical relationship as well as the potential for harm to occur are important features of the definition (Stirling & Kerr, 2008). As such, while the coach may deliberately use harmful coaching practices, there does not need to be an explicit intent to harm the athlete to constitute emotional abuse (Stirling & Kerr, 2008). Examples of emotionally abusive coaching practices include: verbal comments that are humiliating, berating, demeaning or insulting; throwing objects for the purposes of intimidation; and the denial of attention and support (Stirling & Kerr, 2007). Of all forms of maltreatment, including sexual, physical, emotional abuse and neglect, emotionally abusive coaching practices appear to be the most common (Gravely & Cochran, 1995). Alexander, Stafford, and Lewis (2011), in their study of organised sport in the UK, stated that 75% of their sample reportedly experienced emotional harm. As well, Gervis and Dunn (2004) found through semi-structured interviews with 12 former elite child athletes that shouting, belittling, threats and humiliation were commonly experienced. Taken together, the existing literature reveals that athletes commonly report experiences of emotional harm from their coaches.

In addition to the frequent reports of emotionally harmful coaching practices, evidence indicates that these practices are often accepted as a requirement for the development of elite athletes. Coaches and athletes alike interpret such behaviours as an essential element of athlete development (Stirling, 2013; Stirling & Kerr, 2014). More specifically, coaches disclosed that they used emotionally abusive practices in part for instrumental purposes; in other words, they believed these strategies were effective in motivating athletes to enhance their training and performance (Stirling, 2013). Moreover, athletes have also reported that such coaching strategies are helpful in increasing their motivation and signal their coaches' interests in seeing them improve (Stirling & Kerr, 2014). Further, parents of young athletes appear to be socialised into the sport culture to accept emotionally abusive coaching behaviours as an expected practice for athlete development (Kerr & Stirling, 2012). A failure to acknowledge emotionally abusive coaching behaviours as problematic has also been reported amongst other authorities in sport including sport psychology consultants (Stirling & Kerr, 2014) and sport medical practitioners (Stirling, Bridges, Cruz, & Mountjoy, 2011). Ample evidence exists therefore to highlight the normalisation of emotionally abusive coaching practices.

Many potential explanations for the apparent normalisation of emotionally abusive coaching practices have been proposed. Tofler and DiGeronimo (2000), for example, suggest that abusive situations may occur when adults become too absorbed in their own sporting ambitions for their child. The power held by the coach, which has been cited as similar to that held by a priest (Brackenridge, 1997), and a parent (Stirling & Kerr, 2009) is often referenced as influencing the normalisation of questionable practices. Sociological explanations such as the performance narrative (Douglas & Carless, 2006) and the sport ethic (Hughes & Coakley, 1991) which refer to contextual and normative influences such as winning at any cost, unwavering commitment required of athletes, and taking risks and making sacrifices to train and perform have also been proposed to explain the acceptance of harmful coaching practices.

Another potential and as yet unexplored contributor to the normalisation of emotional abuse within the coach–athlete relationship may be the way in which coaches are depicted in the media, specifically in popular films. Many have written about the place and importance of movies within our culture and society's social fabric (Duncan, Nolan, & Wood, 2002; Goldenberg, Lee, & O'Bannon, 2010), and as such, popular films are powerful socialising agents in society (Rogers, 2002). Champoux (1999) cited the value of films as teaching tools as they enable the presentation of material more dramatically than print materials, they can act as a metaphor which often leaves lasting impressions that people can easily recall, they give meaning to concepts, and create strong experiences for viewers. As Safran (1998, p. 227) stated, "film, regardless of its accuracy, serves as a major information source" with much of the information presented in films accepted as factual (Farhi, 1999; Swetnam, 1992).

Within sport, athletes have identified media influences, such as these film portrayals of coach–athlete interactions, as contributing to their acceptance of their own experiences of their coach's emotional abusive practices.

> In sports movies they tend to portray coaches as these people who will have outbursts and go on these rants or throw things, so [it] seemed like it was an acceptable way to act. … We just thought it was him being a coach. (Stirling & Kerr, 2014, p. 125)

The purpose of this study therefore, was to examine film portrayals of coach–athlete interactions in popular, North American, sport films, with a focus on emotional abuse within the coach–athlete relationship. More specifically, this study focused on the types of emotionally abusive coaching behaviours directed at the athlete, the context in which this form of maltreatment occurs, where it occurs, the reasons for its use, precipitating events, timing during the sport season, and the outcome of the experience as depicted in the movie.

Methods

To address the study purpose, a thematic analysis was conducted in which coach–athlete interactions in 19 popular, North American, sport films were analysed with a focus on the portrayal of emotionally abusive behaviours. Thematic analysis refers to the identification and description of implicit and explicit themes reflected in data. It is "useful in capturing the complexities of meaning" and is the most commonly used method in qualitative research (Guest, MacQueen, & Namely, 2012, p. 11).

Inclusion criteria for film selection

Films selected for inclusion in this research were popular English-language sport films within the dramatisation genre, released in the last 25 years, and which included interactions between a coach and an athlete. The film release date range of 1990–2015 was identified as inclusion criteria for this research as during this time period, the formation of the World Wide Web enabled widespread access to information as well as opportunities to watch films more readily and frequently online (Geck, 2006). According to Geck (2006), the generation Z population, representing individuals born as of 1990 and onward, is particularly engaged with and influenced by media messages. This time period represents films that would have been released during the youth and adolescence of many current athletes, a period of development in which imitation and acceptance of media portrayals is prominent (Davidson, Lefebvre, Morris, Nieman, & Swift, 2003; Michel & Roebers, 2008).

This research focused exclusively on films within the dramatisation genre which is characterised by realistic plots, settings, characters and interactions between the characters (Dirks, 2000). Drama, the largest film genre, includes films that are based on everyday social contexts, conflicts and environments that resonate with audiences (Hornaday, 2011). As we were focused on how film portrayals of coach–athlete interactions reflected emotionally abusive behaviours, the film had to include interactions between a coach and an athlete to be included in this study. Films released in the English language were also a prerequisite for inclusion.

Film selection process

Initially, searches for the *best sport movies of all time* were gathered from lists provided by following websites: Fox Sports and ESPN (prominent distributors of sporting news and information), NY Daily News and Rolling Stone Magazine (popular media outlets), and the Internet movie database (IMDb: an extensive database for movie reviews and information). However, when the top rated sport movies were crossed referenced across these sites, there were no consistencies. As a result, movies selected for this review were identified from a reference list of the most frequently searched sports movie titles obtained through the Google Internet search engine. As the premier search engine in North America, these search results served as a proxy for the most popular sport-related films. The initial list of the most frequently searched sport films yielded 50 films. Further refinement of this list against the study inclusion criteria lead to the exclusion of movies that were

Table 1. Movies included in thematic analysis.

Film title	Release date	Sport(s) of focus	Level of sport	Gender of coach(es)	Gender of athlete(s)
Any Given Sunday	1999	Football	Professional	M/ F	M
A League of Their Own	1992	Baseball	Professional	M	F
Bend It Like Beckham	2002	Soccer	Competitive youth	M/ F	F
Blue Chips	1994	Basketball	Intercollegiate	M	M
Coach Carter	2005	Basketball	High school	M	M
Friday Night Lights	2004	Football	High school	M	M
Glory Road	2006	Basketball	Intercollegiate	M	M
He Got Game	1998	Basketball	Recreational/ High school	M	M
Invincible	2006	Football	Professional	M	M
Million Dollar Baby	2004	Boxing	Professional	M/ F	F
Miracle	2004	Hockey	International	M	M
Remember The Titans	2000	Football	High school	M	M
Rudy	1993	Football	Intercollegiate	M	M
The Blind Spot	2009	Football	High school	M	M
The Express	2008	Football	Intercollegiate	M	M
The Mighty Ducks	1992	Hockey	Competitive youth	M	M/ F
The Replacements	2000	Football	Professional	M	M
Varsity Blues	1999	Football	High school	M	M
We Are Marshall	2006	Football	Intercollegiate	M	M

released prior to 1990 (20 films were excluded), films that did not involve some form of coaching (3 were excluded), documentary style films (2 were excluded) and comedic films (6 were excluded), resulting in a total of 19 movies. Film titles and descriptive features are summarised in Table 1.

Thematic analysis

A confirmatory thematic approach was employed for the analysis of the data. Films were reviewed in full and themes of information were coded deductively relative to pre-determined analysis categories. These categories were determined based upon previous literature on athletes' experiences of emotional abuse in sport – in particular, literature describing athletes' experiences of emotional abuse in the coach–athlete relationship (Stirling & Kerr, 2007, 2014), the reasons for use of emotionally abusive coaching practices (Stirling, 2013), types of emotionally abusive behaviours (Stirling & Kerr, 2008) and potential outcomes of emotional abuse in sport (Stirling & Kerr, 2013). More specifically, the categorisation of behaviours portrayed in the films was conducted in congruence with previous research that has highlighted three forms of emotionally abusive coaching behaviours: (i) verbal behaviours including yelling, berating, name-calling, intimidating and humiliating comments; (ii) physical behaviours such as throwing objects to intimidate (not to strike the athlete); and (iii) the denial of attention and support such as ignoring an athlete until she or he performs as expected (Stirling & Kerr, 2008). The categorisation of reasons for a coach's use of such behaviours was aligned with previously documented reasons as either expressive – when a coach loses emotional control –or as instrumental – when a coach believes these behaviours will enhance the athlete's performance (Stirling, 2013). And finally, previously reported athletes' responses to emotionally abusive coaching behaviours, including effects on motivation and performance as examples (Stirling & Kerr, 2013), were used to analyse the films.

Each film was coded individually and coded themes within each category and sub-category of analysis were totalled across all films reviewed. Data were then analysed descriptively to illustrate a representation of the theme relative to the total number of incidents of emotionally abusive practices between a coach and an athlete as portrayed in the sport films reviewed. Thematic analysis of the coded themes was discussed and categorised by a group of three researchers to assure trustworthiness in this process.

Results

Across the 19 films examined, a total of 346 incidents of emotionally abusive interactions between a coach and an athlete were documented. Consistent with the categories of analysis examined, results are presented under the main themes of: sport-related features (sport), descriptive factors of the perpetrator and recipient (who), environmental context (where), types of emotionally abusive behaviours portrayed (what), reasons for use (why), timing (when), and outcomes and responses (what happened next). Each theme will be reviewed in turn.

Sport-related features

Of the 346 incidents recorded, 95.6% of the incidents ($n = 331$) occurred in team sport contexts (i.e. baseball, basketball, football, hockey, soccer) and 4.3% of the incidents ($n = 11$) occurred in the context of an individual sport (i.e. boxing). Incidents of emotionally abusive coaching practices were portrayed at varying levels of sport including professional sport (26%; $n = 90$), international sport (5.8%; $n = 20$), intercollegiate sporting contexts (25.1%; $n = 87$), high school sport (31.4%; $n = 109$), and within competitive youth (8.7%; $n = 30$) and recreational sporting contexts (2.9%; $n = 10$).

Descriptive factors of the perpetrator and recipient

Of the 346 emotionally abusive interactions recorded, the most frequent perpetrator of the harmful practices, as recorded in 68.2% ($n = 236$) of the incidents, was the head coach, followed by peers (9.9%; $n = 34$), parents (6.6%; $n = 23$), the assistant coach (6.1%, $n = 21$), fans (3.8%, $n = 13$), the team manager (2.3%; $n = 8$) and the sports agent (1.2%; $n = 4$). In the remaining 2% ($n = 7$) of the incidents recorded, the use of the harmful practice was not specific to one person.

Athletes were the portrayed recipient of the emotionally harmful practices in the majority of the incidents recorded (85%; $n = 294$). Other recipients included head coaches (4%; $n = 14$) assistant coaches (2.9%; $n = 10$), team managers (1.7%;

$n = 6$), fans (1.7%; $n = 6$), parents (0.3%; $n = 1$) and a sport agent (0.3%; $n = 1$). The remaining 4.3% ($n = 15$) were not specific to one recipient.

In 96.8% ($n = 335$) of the emotionally abusive interactions recorded, a male directed the harmful behaviour. The emotionally abusive behaviour was directed by a female in 3.2% ($n = 11$) of the incidents recorded. Eighty-eight per cent ($n = 305$) of males and 11.8% ($n = 41$) of females were recipients of the emotionally abusive behaviour.

Environmental context

The majority of emotionally abusive interactions (67.9%; $n = 235$) occurred at an athletic venue (i.e. field of play, gymnasium). Other locations included the locker room (16.2%; $n = 56$), home (8.7%; $n = 30$), vehicle (3.2%; $n = 11$) and classroom (0.9%; $n = 3$). The remaining 3.17% ($n = 11$) was not specific to one location.

Incidents of emotionally abusive interactions occurred either in a group or individual setting. In the group setting, the emotionally abusive behaviour was directed at more than one individual at a time (e.g. behaviour directed at the entire team); whereas, in the individual setting, the behaviour was directed towards one person. Of the 346 incidents recorded, 32.9% ($n = 114$) occurred in a group setting and 67.1% ($n = 232$) occurred in an individual setting.

The emotionally harmful interactions were also portrayed as occurring in both public (47.7%; $n = 165$) and private (52.3%; $n = 181$) contexts. Regardless of whether the harmful interaction occurred publically or privately, a bystander was present and observed the interaction (e.g. coaches, parents, teammates, fans, peers) in 78.6% ($n = 272$) of the incidents.

Types of emotionally abusive behaviours portrayed

Interactions that were interpreted as being emotionally-abusive were portrayed in the films as verbal behaviours (86.1%; $n = 298$), physical behaviours (35.8%; $n = 124$), and the denial of attention and support (16.2%; $n = 56$). Of the harmful verbal behaviours portrayed ($n = 298$), all of the interactions were direct verbal interactions where the comments made were directly about the recipient. In a few of the incidents (5%; $n = 15$) indirect verbal comments were also made about the recipient's friends and/or family. The harmful verbal behaviours most frequently portrayed were yelling (61.4%; $n = 248$) and demeaning comments (54.3%; $n = 188$), followed by name-calling (41.2%; $n = 139$), negative comparison (26.9%; $n = 93$) and threatening comments (21.1%; $n = 73$). Some examples of the verbal comments made by head coaches to players included "You're playing like the village idiot! You want people to think of you as the village idiot?" (*Friday Night Lights*) and "Cry me a river, you fat fucking baby!" (*Varsity Blues*).

Of the harmful physical behaviours portrayed ($n = 124$), 57.6% ($n = 71$) were contact physical behaviours such as pushing ($n = 44$), slapping ($n = 37$) and punching ($n = 33$). Similarly, 47% ($n = 70$) were non-contact behaviours including excessive exercise ($n = 41$), hitting or throwing objects ($n = 19$) and prolonged stretching/motionlessness ($n = 14$). As both contact and non-contact behaviours were used by the perpetrator in some incidents, the percentages total more than 100%. Although some of these behaviours may also be classified as physically abusive, they also have potential to be emotionally harmful. As an example, in the movie *Coach Carter*, the head coach told the players that "if you are late you will run. If you give me attitude you will do push-ups. So you can push-up or shutup!" Similarly, in the movie, *Remember the Titans*, the coach tells the team:

> We will be perfect in every aspect of the game. You drop a pass, you run a mile. You miss a blocking assignment, you run a mile. You fumble the football, and I will break my foot off in your John Brown hind parts and then you will run a mile.

The denial of attention and support was the least frequently portrayed form of emotionally harmful behaviour. Of the 346 total incidents recorded in the films, benching occurred in 6.9% ($n = 24$) of the incidents. The denial of rest/water was viewed in 6.6% of the incidents ($n = 23$) and the lack of praise/recognition occurred in 6.4% ($n = 22$) of the incidents recorded.

Reasons for use

Based upon the film plot and the circumstances surrounding the emotionally abusive interactions, reasons identified for the use of the harmful behaviours included: expressive reasons (70.5%; $n = 244$) in which the emotionally abusive interaction transpired from a lack of regulation of feelings of anger and/or frustration; punishment reasons (15.2%; $n = 52$) where the behaviour was used to enforce or alter the behaviour of the recipient; and for performance enhancement (30.3%; $n = 105$) or a strategy to enhance the athletic performance capabilities of the recipient. In 6.9% ($n = 24$) of the incidents, the reason for the incident was not clear.

The most commonly reported events that precipitated the 346 emotionally abusive interactions included: poor performance (32%; $n = 110$), a sport-related error/mistake (22%; $n = 76$), disruptive behaviour (19%; $n = 65$) on the part of the recipient (e.g. talking during practice), not paying attention (12%; $n = 41$), and poor attitude (12%; $n = 40$).

Timing

Across the 19 films, four distinct time periods were identified in which the emotionally abusive interactions occurred. Of the 346 incidents recorded, 52.3% ($n = 181$) occurred during training and 36% ($n = 125$) occurred during competition. Six per cent of the incidents ($n = 21$) occurred during off-season and 5.5% ($n = 19$) occurred during recruitment or tryouts.

Outcomes and responses

After experiencing an emotionally abusive interaction, the most common response demonstrated by recipients was an emotional one (60.4%; n = 209). Verbal and non-verbal displays of the recipients were interpreted as representing the following emotional responses: sadness (n = 155), anger (n = 92), fear/anxiety (n = 106), irritation (n = 41), low self-efficacy (n = 5), low self-esteem (n = 9), enhanced morale (n = 27) and decreased morale (n = 86). Following some incidents, more than one emotional response was observed.

The recipients also demonstrated behavioural (24.6%; n = 85) and physical responses (7.5%; n = 26) to emotionally abusive interactions. Behavioural responses included: increased effort in sport (n = 40), passivity (n = 35), decreased effort in sport (n = 19), confrontation (n = 17) and avoidance (n = 1). Physical responses included: exhaustion (n = 26) and vomiting (n = 21), as well as successful performance (n = 9) and sport-specific skill acquisition (n = 4). In the remaining incidents (n = 26) there was no observable response.

Discussion

To reiterate, the purpose of this study was to explore the ways in which popular, North American, sport films portray emotionally abusive interactions within the coach–athlete relationship. Taken together, the findings indicate that emotionally abusive coaching practices are frequently portrayed in sport films through verbal comments, contact and non-contact physical behaviours, and the denial of attention and support. The finding that 346 emotionally abusive occurrences were documented across 19 films highlights and supports existing research that illustrates the common use of emotionally abusive practices (Alexander et al., 2011).

Interestingly, 96% of all documented incidences were portrayed within team sports. This finding should be interpreted with caution however considering that only one of the 19 films reviewed focused on an individual sport. Researchers have reported previously that emotionally abusive coaching practices are employed in individual sports as well, including gymnastics, swimming, track and field, and tennis (Alexander et al., 2011; Stirling & Kerr, 2007, 2008, 2014). A minority of occurrences in these films were either directed at or perpetrated by females, a finding that may be interpreted as supporting the masculine, hegemonic view of sport culture (Messner, Duncan, & Jensen, 1993). This raises questions about the degree to which males and females may relate to the film portrayals and the potential influences of these film depictions on their real-life experiences of emotional abuse in the coach–athlete relationship. Interestingly, the existing research on the effects of aggression in the media has been conducted on males primarily and little is known about females' responses to aggression in the media (Anderson & Murphy, 2003).

To-date, the majority of studies on emotional abuse in the coach–athlete relationship have focused on elite or highly competitive organised sport settings. The findings of this study however, which indicate that the highest percentage of incidences occur within high school sport teams, suggest that researchers should focus future work on this setting. Could it be that emotionally abusive coaching practices are prevalent in high school sport contexts and sport films are simply portraying this reality? Moreover, to what degree do such portrayals influence the normalisation of experiences of emotional abuse at the high school level of sport, particularly given the impressionable qualities of adolescents? To-date, these questions remain unexplored.

Interestingly, 57% of all incidents of emotionally abusive coaching practices portrayed in the films occurred within educational settings, including high school and university/college sports. From this finding, questions arise about the role and purpose of sport within the educational mandate of these institutions. Assuming that emotionally abusive teaching practices in the classroom are not permitted in these institutions, it is perplexing that such methods are so commonly portrayed in school sports. The discernible qualities associated with the portrayals of school sport coaches raise questions about the contextual considerations that may be unique to this setting and that may contribute to the acceptance of such abusive practices.

The finding that bystanders were present and observed 79% of the documented emotionally abusive incidents without intervening, lends support to the proposition that emotionally abusive coaching practices are normalised. Many of these bystanders included parents and other coaches who are in positions of authority and responsibility to care for the well-being of young people; by not responding to or intervening in such abusive practices, they are, in effect, complicit in the abuse. The lack of intervention sends the message that such abusive coaching conduct is acceptable. Previous researchers have referred to 'passive bystanders' as those who observe violence and do not intervene; these individuals are often perceived by victims to be in collusion with an abuser even though they may not be directly involved with the abusive conduct (Gini, Pozzoli, Borghi, & Franzoni, 2008). Some of the conditions identified as facilitating intervention by bystanders include: being aware that something is occurring; interpreting the event as not something innocuous; taking responsibility for intervening; knowing how to intervene; and making a decision to intervene (Latane & Darley, 1970). One may deduce that if adults in the sport context do not appraise coaching behaviours as problematic then there is no need to take responsibility for intervening. Others have highlighted the importance of contextual factors in contributing to one's inclination to intervene (Pozzoli & Gini, 2013); as such, an ecological approach to understanding the facilitators and barriers to intervening with abusive coaches represents an interesting direction for future research.

Of all forms of emotionally abusive coaching practices, the use of verbal behaviours (86%) in the forms of yelling and negative comments appears to predominate.

In a similar study, McCullick, Belcher, Hardin, and Hardin (2003) reported that physical education teachers are typically portrayed in popular movies as bullies who seem to enjoy humiliating, berating and embarrassing students, verbally. The common use of emotionally abusive verbal behaviours such as yelling and negative comments is also consistent with previous research on the coach–athlete relationship (Gervis & Dunn, 2004; Stirling & Kerr, 2008).

Physical behaviours (36%) such as administering exercise as punishment and throwing objects in anger or frustration were also observed. Similarly, McCullick et al. (2003) found that physical education teachers were portrayed in movies as throwing objects and using exercise as punishment as consequences for undesirable behaviours. Interestingly, in their analyses, these authors reported that no clear distinctions were made between the roles physical education teachers play as teachers vs. coaches. Empirical evidence is emerging with respect to the use of exercise as a form of punishment. Burak, Rosenthal, and Richardson (2013) found that more than 90 and 43% of their participants ($n = 345$) reported that their coaches and physical education teachers, respectively, had used exercise to punish or manage behaviour. Although the use of excessive exercise may cause physical harm, it is included here as a form of emotional abuse by virtue of the potential for athletes to feel subservient, humiliated and degraded. Despite the proliferation of policies denouncing the use of exercise as punishment (e.g. Canadian Centre for Ethics in Sport, 2013; National Association for Sport and Physical Education, 2009), this position is not reflected in the films.

Coaches were recorded as denying attention and support to a lesser degree than the other emotionally abusive practices (16%). Representative behaviours included benching, and denying athletes praise, recognition, rest and water, consistent with previous literature (Stirling & Kerr, 2008). With the increasing public media attention devoted to the death of athletes as a result of excessive exercise without proper hydration (Binkley, Beckett, Casa, Kleiner, & Plummer, 2002), it is particularly disconcerting that these behaviours are portrayed in these films as standard coaching practices.

The perceived reasons for the use of emotionally abusive coaching practices included: anger/frustration, performance enhancement and punishment purposes. These findings are consistent with Stirling's (2013) research in which coaches purported to use emotionally abusive coaching practices as functions of losing emotional control (expressive reasons) and a belief that such strategies enhanced athletes' motivation and performance (instrumental reasons).

Although this study did not assess the influence of these portrayals on observers' views or acceptance of these abusive practices, it is plausible that cinematic depictions of coaches influence the normalisation of emotionally abusive coaching strategies, a proposition based upon social cognitive theory. According to this theory, people learn, in part, through the observations of others' behaviours and whether these behaviours are associated with rewards or punishments (Bandura, 1986). When individuals observe others and the consequences of others' behaviours, either in-person or through film representations, they learn and use these observations to guide their own behaviour. The media provides a vast array of diverse opportunities to learn through the observation of others and has been shown to influence attitudes and beliefs (Baran & David, 2000). Wadsworth (1998) for example, criticised negative depictions of teachers in the media as influencing unfavourable perceptions about education. When viewers watch film portrayals of charismatic, winning coaches engage in emotionally abusive practices without intervention or punishment, and who more often than not, are glorified for such behaviours, important messages are conveyed about the acceptability of these practices.

The consequences of exposure to aggression and violence in the media may be gradual and cumulative (Krahe, 2012) and may facilitate desensitisation to aggression over time (Bushman & Anderson, 2009; Krahe, 2012; Ostrow, Gentile, & Crick, 2006). As an example, Yang and Huesman (2013) argued that children whose families watched television together were more likely to adopt the attitudes and values portrayed in the television shows, including acceptance of violence. Could it be therefore, that watching film portrayals of coaches engaging in emotionally abusive practices may desensitise viewers to these forms of aggression and thus contribute to normalisation? This is an important question for future research.

The reported findings of this study are limited by the choice of films; for example, the 25 year time period was arbitrary and given the accessibility of older films, it is possible that viewers watch films made outside of this timeframe such as *Rocky* on repeated occasions across time. The study is also limited by the subjectivity and lack of triangulation regarding the classification of behaviours portrayed in the films. While this study explored the portrayal of emotional abuse in sport films, it did not examine the scope of such abuse. Further, future research would benefit from delving into questions about who wrote, produced and directed these films and for which audiences, questions that are undoubtedly related to the paucity of films made about female athletes and female coaches.

In summary, the prevalence of occurrences of emotionally abusive coaching practices in the selected films suggests that such practices are typically associated with sport coaching. Further, the finding that bystanders are present in the majority of occurrences and do not intervene suggests these behaviours are normalised in this context; therefore, future research should explore interventions by which abusive behaviours can be identified as such and addressed.

Disclosure statement

No potential conflict of interest was reported by the authors.

References

Alexander, K., & Stafford, A., & Lewis, R. (2011). *The experiences of children participating in organized sport in the UK*. London/NSPCC Child Protection Research Unit.

Anderson, C., & Murphy, C. (2003). Violent video games and aggressive behavior in young women. *Aggressive Behavior, 29*, 423–429.

Bandura, A. (1986). *Social foundations of thought and action: A social cognitive theory*. Englewood Cliffs, NJ: Prentice-Hall.

Baran, J., & David, D. (2000). *Mass communication theory: Foundations, ferment and future*. Belmont, CA: Wadsworth.

Binkley, H., Beckett, J., Casa, D., Kleiner, D., & Plummer, P. (2002). National athletic trainers' association position statement: Exertional heat illnesses. *Journal of Athletic Training, 37*, 329–343.

Brackenridge, C. H. (1997). 'He owned me basically...' Women's experience of sexual abuse in sport. *International Review for the Sociology of Sport, 32*, 115–130.

Burak, L., Rosenthal, M., & Richardson, K. (2013). Examining attitudes, beliefs, and intentions regarding the use of exercise as punishment in physical education and sport: An application of the theory of reasoned action. *Journal of Applied Social Psychology, 43*, 1436–1445.

Bushman, B., & Anderson, C. (2009). Comfortably numb: Desensitizing effects of violent media on helping others. *Psychological Science, 20*, 273–277.

Canadian Centre for Ethics in Sport. (2013). *The use of physical punishment of children and youth in sport and recreation*. Retrieved from http://www.cces.ca/files/pdfs/CCESPositionStatementonUseofPhysicalPunishment_English.pdf

Champoux, J. (1999). Film as a teaching resource. *Journal of Management Inquiry, 8*, 206–217.

Crooks, C. V., & Wolfe, D. A. (2007). Child abuse and neglect. In E. J. Mash & R. A. Barkley (Eds.), *Assessment of childhood disorders* (4th ed., pp. 639–684). New York, NY: Guilford Press.

Davidson, S., Lefebvre, A., Morris, P., Nieman, P., & Swift, C. (2003). Putting media under the microscope: Understanding and challenging media's influence on the health and well-being of children and youth. *Paediatrics & Child Health, 8*, 265–266.

Dirks, T. (2000). *Main film genres*. Retrieved from http://www.filmsite.org/genres.html

Douglas, K., & Carless, D. (2006). Performance, discovery, and relational narratives among women professional tournament golfers. *Women in Sport and Physical Activity Journal, 15*, 14–27.

Duncan, C., Nolan, J., & Wood, R. (2002). See you in the movies? We hope not! *Journal of Physical Education, Recreation & Dance, 73*, 38–44.

Farhi, A. (1999). Hollywood goes to school: Recognizing the super teacher myth in film. *The Clearing House: A Journal of Educational Strategies, Issues and Ideas, 72*, 157–159.

Geck, A. (2006). The generation Z connection: Teaching information literacy to the Newest net generation. In E. Rosenfeld & D. Loertscher (Eds.), *Toward a 21st century school library media program* (pp. 236–241). Lanham, MD: Scarecrow Press.

Gervis, M., & Dunn, N. (2004). The emotional abuse of elite child athletes by their coaches. *Child Abuse Review, 13*, 215–223.

Gini, G., Pozzoli, T., Borghi, F., & Franzoni, L. (2008). The role of bystanders in students' perception of bullying and sense of safety. *Journal of School Psychology, 46*, 617–638.

Glaser, D. (2002). Emotional abuse and neglect (psychological maltreatment): A conceptual framework. *Child Abuse & Neglect, 26*, 697–714.

Goldenberg, M., Lee, J., & O'Bannon, T. (2010). Enhancing recreation, parks and tourism courses: Using movies as teaching tools. *Journal of Hospitality, Leisure, Sport & Tourism Education, 9*, 4–16.

Gravely, A. R., & Cochran, T. R. (1995, May 28–31). *The use of perceptual data to assess intercollegiate athletics.* Paper presented at the 35th Annual Forum of the Association for Institutional Research, Boston, MA.

Guest, G., MacQueen, K. M., & Namely, E. E. (2012). *Applied thematic analysis.* Thousand Oaks, CA: Sage.

Hornaday, A. (2011). Today's movies deliver more realistic, gritty everyday scenes. *The Washington Post.* Retrieved September, 30, 2015 from http://www.washingtonpost.com/wp-dyn/content/article/2011/01/06/AR2011010605897.html?sid=ST2011010606287

Hughes, R., & Coakley, J. (1991). Positive deviance among athletes: The implications of over-conformity to the sport ethic. *Sociology of Sport Journal, 8,* 307–325.

Kerr, G. A., & Stirling, A. E. (2012). Parents' reflections on their child's experiences of emotionally abusive coaching practices. *Journal of Applied Sport Psychology, 24,* 191–206.

Krahe, B. (2012). Report of the media violence commission. *Aggressive Behavior, 38,* 335–341.

Latane, B., & Darley, J. M. (1970). *The unresponsive bystander: Why doesn't he help?* New York, NY: Appleton-Century-Crofts.

McCullick, B., Belcher, D., Hardin, B., & Hardin, M. (2003). Butches, bullies and buffoons: Images of physical education teachers in the movies. *Sport, Education and Society, 8,* 3–16.

Messner, M. A., Duncan, M. C., & Jensen, K. (1993). Separating the men from the girls: The gendered language of televised sports. *Gender & Society, 7,* 121–137.

Michel, E., & Roebers, C. M. (2008). Children's knowledge acquisition through film: Influence of programme characteristics. *Applied Cognitive Psychology, 22,* 1228–1244.

National Association for Sport and Physical Education. (2009). Physical activity used as punishment and/or behavior management. [Position statement]. Retrieved from http://www.aahperd.org/naspe/standards/upload/Physical-Activity-as-Punishment-to-Board-12-10.pdf

Orlick, T. D., & Boterill, C. (1975). *Every kid can win.* Chicago, IL: Nelson Hall.

Ostrow, J., Gentile, D., & Crick, N. (2006). Media exposure, aggression and prosocial behavior during early childhood: A longitudinal study. *Social Development, 15,* 612–627.

Pozzoli, T., & Gini, G. (2013). Why do bystanders of bullying help or not? A multidimensional model. *The Journal of Early Adolescence, 33,* 315–340.

Rogers, E. (2002). *Waiting to exhale: African American women and adult learning through movies.* Paper presented at the 43rd Annual Meeting of the Adult Education Research Conference, Raleigh, NC.

Ryan, J. (2005). *Little girls in pretty boxes: The making and breaking of elite gymnasts and figure skaters.* London: The Women's Press.

Safran, S. P. (1998). Disability portrayal in film: Reflecting the past, directing the future. *Exceptional Children, 64,* 227–238.

Stirling, A. E. (2013). Understanding the use of emotionally abusive coaching practices. *International Journal of Sports Science & Coaching, 8,* 625–639.

Stirling, A. E., Bridges, E., Cruz, E. L., & Mountjoy, M. (2011). Canadian academy of sport and exercise medicine position paper: Abuse, harassment, and bullying in sport. *Clinical Journal of Sport Medicine, 21,* 385–391.

Stirling, A. E., & Kerr, G. A. (2007). Elite female swimmers' experiences of emotional abuse across time. *Journal of Emotional Abuse, 7,* 89–113.

Stirling, A. E., & Kerr, G. A. (2008). Defining and categorizing emotional abuse in sport. *European Journal of Sport Science, 8,* 173–181.

Stirling, A. E., & Kerr, G. A. (2009). Abused athletes' perceptions of the coach–athlete relationship. *Sport in Society, 12,* 227–239.

Stirling, A. E., & Kerr, G. (2013). The perceived effects of elite athletes' experiences of emotional abuse in the coach–athlete relationship. *International Journal of Sport and Exercise Psychology, 11,* 87–100.

Stirling, A. E., & Kerr, G. (2014). Initiating and sustaining emotional abuse in the coach–athlete relationship: An ecological transactional model of vulnerability. *Journal of Aggression, Maltreatment & Trauma, 23*, 116–125.

Swetnam, L. A. (1992). Media distortion of the teacher image. *The Clearing House: A Journal of Educational Strategies, Issues and Ideas, 66*, 30–32.

Tofler, I., & DiGeronimo, T. F. (2000). *Keeping your kids out front without kicking them from behind: How to nurture high-achieving athletes, scholars, and performing artists*. San Francisco, CA: Jossey-Bass.

Wachtel, A. (1999). *The state of the art in child abuse prevention*. Ottawa: Health Canada.

Wadsworth, D. (1998). Do media shape public perceptions of American school? In G. Maeroff (Ed.), *Imaging education: The media and school in America* (pp. 59–68). New York, NY: Teacher's College Press.

Yang, G., & Huesman, L. (2013). Correlates of media habits across time, generations, and media modalities. *Journal of Broadcasting & Electronic Media, 57*, 356–373.

Too hot to handle? A social semiotic analysis of touching in *"Bend it like Beckham"*

Dean Garratt[a] and Heather Piper[b]

[a]Faculty of Education and Children's Services, University of Chester, Manchester, UK; [b]Education and Social Research Institute, Manchester Metropolitan University, Manchester, UK

ABSTRACT

This article examines the cinematic portrayal of touching and its politics in sports coaching, exploring how social interactions between coach and athlete are symbolically represented. The analysis focuses primarily on a well-known British-produced film, *Bend it like Beckham* (2002), in which scenes exhibit different forms of touching. The construction of intimate coach–athlete relationships captured through a series of filmed encounters is analysed through a social semiotic frame. This requires judgements about the authority, "reality-status" and possibility of meaning arising from such representational practices. Attention is drawn to different moments of intimacy and/or sexual tension between the lead coach and central female characters, both on and off the pitch. Through a series of detailed interpretations, we show how the complexities involved in assigning intentionality in cinematic contexts serves both to assert and displace meaning. This further problematises moral aspects of relations between coaches and athletes in tactile encounters, and especially so within the context of risk-averse safeguarding policies in sports coaching, a context characterised by increased prescription, proscription and disciplinary intervention during the years since the film was released.

Introduction

In a series of articles (Garratt and Piper, 2014; Garratt, Piper, & Taylor, 2013; Piper, Garratt, & Taylor, 2013; Piper, Taylor, & Garratt, 2012), relating to a recently completed ESRC project, *Hands off sports coaching: the politics of touch* (RES000-22-4156; Piper & Garratt, 2012), we discussed the practical impact and moral significance of safeguarding and child protection policy in contemporary coaching practice. We argued that the wide, pervasive and moral crusader-led discourse of safeguarding and child protection has created a "folk devil" and moral panic (Cohen, 1999; Piper, 2014), escalating fear among coaches and radically disturbing the role of the coach through the adoption of questionable defensive and self-protective practices (Taylor, Piper, & Garratt, 2014). This has corollary implications and often deleterious consequences for the development of sound intergenerational relationships between coach and athlete in youth sport and physical education, alongside collateral negative effects in adult sport.

It is relevant here that in the U.K., young people from the age of 16 are able to make their own choices about their sexual partners, unless the other person is acting *in loco parentis*, for example, as their teacher. In such situations, regulations place any adult engaging in improper contact with one of their charges at risk of professional damage and in some cases prosecution. In recent decades, this approach has been extended to a wider group of workers including sports coaches. Increasingly, sports have moved in this direction; coaches being given written and/or verbal guidelines by their clubs, prohibiting touching and personal relationships with young athletes (see Piper & Garratt, 2012; for evidence). This means that regulations originally intended for children have become guidelines which increasingly apply to (usually) young adult women, even into their mid-20s (see McRae & Pendleton, 2012). These damaging trends are significant, especially given the influence of particular policy antecedents in relation to youth sport and contemporary coaching practice. Previously, adopting a Foucauldian genealogical approach (Foucault, 1991), we traced the social and historical formation of safeguarding policy and examined its pervasive influence in the wider social and political context in which contemporary practices of coaching have systematically emerged and discursively developed (Garratt et al., 2013). However, while this analysis drew critical attention to the malign effect of policy *discourse* and *statements* upon the construction and configuration of coaching relations, regulations and moral prohibitions, it did not specifically examine social semiotic activity; that is, *signs* through the interactions occurring between coach and athlete. By this we refer to the way in which semiotic resources (Jewitt & Oyama, 2001) can be utilised to analyse the *potential* meanings deriving from social interaction, where such affordances (Gibson, 1979) exceed but do not exclude the written and/or spoken word. We are thus proposing a synergy that brings social semiotics into dialogue with Foucauldian notions of discourse, power/knowledge and governmentality. The importance of social context and interaction as part of a broader communicative repertoire is entirely congruent with a Foucauldian frame in which networks of social relations speak persuasively to discursive *practices* as opposed to mere statements alone.

Thus, it is through this semiotic frame that we envision and locate this article, critically examining the way in which social interactions between coach and athlete are symbolically represented. We consider how this visual representation, conveying a morality of relations and tactile encounters, is socially regulated and explore how this may serve to perpetuate risk-averse practice in sports coaching. A key point of departure for our analysis is the understanding that all discourse and resources for representation are conceived as socially plural, with the potential to produce nuanced interpretations of "reality" that are always already socially and culturally riven and produced. This approach is in harmony with Barthes's (1977) concept of *polysemy* in which all images are essentially unstable, comprising multiple layers that are sensitive to contextual debate. In this way, our interpretation of cinematic contexts emerges from a cultural reference point that is inevitably partial and incomplete. Our limited interpretations thus invoke the rich and diverse nature of "reality", adding value through an intertextuality that connects to everything outside the film: the broader cultural milieu. This is pertinent as we redeploy the concept of genealogy as a means to locate and interpret competing discourses and practices of non-verbal interactions. Through this multimodal frame we show how, in seeking to understand issues around safeguarding in the power-asymmetric context of sports coaching, *Bend it like Beckham* remains a significant cinematic resource. The story is not merely anchored to the time of its making; rather, it is effected contemporaneously in the process of its viewing.

Bend it like Beckham

The film combines drama, romance and comedy, and foregrounds association football and the ambition of two young women living in Hounslow, west London to become professional players. Traditionally masculine and male-dominated, football is used as a theme to challenge a range of prominent social issues, including homophobia, gender and cultural stereotyping and, in particular, the role of women in society against a backdrop of conflicting social, cultural, and religious values and practices. The film's title references the renowned footballer David Beckham (then near his peak) and his trademark success in scoring spectacular goals from free kicks, "bending" the ball at speed around the opponents' defensive wall. The film deploys this emblematically as a mark of excellence, an aspirational target for anyone seeking to become a professional footballer. The story revolves around the friendship of two 18-year-old females, Jess (Jesminder) and Jules (Juliette), from contrasting ethnic and cultural backgrounds. Jess is the daughter of Punjabi-Sikh Indian parents, who prove to have serious qualms as to whether football is a suitable interest or career for their younger daughter. She has a passion for football (and David Beckham) and often plays in the park with her friend Tony and his mates. Here she is observed, and her talent for running at speed around opponents with the ball at her feet recognised, by Jules who already plays for the local women's team, Hounslow Harriers. Jules persuades Jess to try out for the team, which is coached by Joe (a man of Irish descent, in his mid-20s) who is impressed by her skills and recruits her. Subsequently, Jess and Jules become best friends in spite of an emerging tension: both are attracted to Joe. This builds throughout the film, in verbal and non-verbal ways, sparking anxiety, ambiguity and anticipation between the three central characters. As this three-way relationship deepens, the politics of "touching" (both literally and metaphorically) becomes increasingly prominent and notions of appropriate and inappropriate behaviour in coach–athlete relationships are rendered ambiguous.

Rationale and conceptual frame

Our selection of *Bend it like Beckham* is significant for two reasons. First, beyond its original high-profile and box office success, it has attracted critical and analytic attention from a wide variety of interdisciplinary perspectives and academic areas. These include those focusing on: the semiotics of cultural difference and cultural translation in cinema (Roy, 2006); racialised experiences of gender and identity in women's football (Ratna, 2011); identity politics and postcolonial feminism (Donnell, 2007); the politics of racial performativity (Giardina, 2003); representations of women's sexuality (Caudwell, 2009); and the relationship between motor behaviours and observed actions in famous athletes (Bach & Tipper, 2006). However, despite this diverse and eclectic response, none have applied a social semiotic frame to the process of understanding the film's treatment of the politics of touch in coaching. Thus, building on our previous research experience in the area, by taking a critical look at the morality of cinematically portrayed tactile encounters in intimate coach–athlete relationships, we present a novel contribution to the field. Secondly, while our choice of *Bend it like Beckham* (released in April 2002) may seem dated, it is entirely deliberate. As Jewitt and Oyama (2001) affirm, "semiotic resources are at once the products of cultural histories and the cognitive resources we use to create meaning in the production and interpretation of visual and other messages" (p. 136). This film has particular historical resonance, supporting understanding of the contemporary politics of touching behaviour in sports coaching. Its moral and political genealogy conveys both discontinuity and continuity in relation to a range of prevalent prohibitive discourses of the early 2000s.

In a Foucauldian sense, *Bend it like Beckham* can be read to symbolise a type of social authority or "governmentality" (Foucault, 1979), its resource and potentiality prompting the "invention" of specific interests and purposes (Jewitt & Oyama, 2001) in a particular cultural context. Thus, its fictional status reflects reality's cultural preconceptions and, from a particular "point of view" (Kress & van Leeuwen, 1996), simultaneously produces them as naturalised. Cinematic representations of touching thus produce an "effect of power" (Foucault, 2002a), with a disciplinary function which serves to structure the "conduct of conduct" (Foucault, 1983). This is where the exercise of power, exerted as a mechanism of coercion, serves as a guide to influence action across a field of possibilities by putting in place the possible outcome. Power is thus understood as less an obvious confrontation and more as a subtly nuanced concept of government (Foucault, 2002a, p. 341). Mapping onto film as a medium and technology of governmentality, visual images may thus prove persuasive in educating people to conduct themselves in particular ways. In turn, the film also conveys a "relational modality" (Foucault, 2002b, p. 59) and hence intertextuality, its conceptual reach cutting across multiple social, cultural and political boundaries and further contributing to the production of a generalised politics of what counts as "true" (Foucault, 1980). In part this "regime of truth" is reactive, shaped in the U.K. sports coaching and child protection context by other pervasive and ubiquitous prohibitions, authoritative statements and policy documents (The Stationery Office [TSO], 1996a; The Stationery Office (TSO), 1996b; Department of Health (DoH), 1999) and other relevant legislation. Also significant is the inauguration in 2001 of the Child Protection in Sport Unit (CPSU) as a department of the National Society for the Prevention of Cruelty to Children, partly funded by national sports organisations.

Collateral developments included the introduction of the Criminal Record Bureau under part five, section 113 of the Police Act 1997 (www.legislation.gov.uk), and the necessity of checks on all adults in a position of authority and care over children or vulnerable others, formally introduced just a month before the release of the film. Thus, in this social and political context, *Bend it like Beckham* can be seen to represent a potentially powerful symbolic device. It projects a cinematic representation of the moral ambiguity around touching at a time when panic and fear around intergenerational and power-asymmetric relationships was beginning to escalate and be subject to critical analysis (Furedi, 2002; Piper et al., 2012). However, at this time such uncertainty was being discursively played out with seemingly untroubled authority and confidence, as the impact of disciplinary regulations and guidelines had not yet been recognised.

In what follows we discuss six scenes, in the order they occur in the film. They are selected for the way in which they capture and illuminate elements of the moral ambience and ambiguity to which we refer; they verbally and visually represent and symbolise the apparent tensions and contradictions in touching behaviours between coach and athletes. The selective nature of the process, in terms of the scenes we have chosen to privilege, is unavoidable. These reflect our "point of view" (Kress & van Leeuwen, 1996), or authorial omnipotence that reflexively positions us, constructing a field of action consisting of potential meanings and symbolic relations. Kvale's (2008) point about interviews is relevant, here applied to the context of visual analysis: "transcripts are not copies or representations of some original reality, they are interpretative constructions that are useful tools for given purposes" (p. 98). Conceived as a semiotic resource, we recognise that our interpretation of the film can thus be read in a variety of ways, in which interpretations resist any final meaning or fixed ontological status.

Social semiotics, interpretation and moral ambiguity

Selection one

Following her trial for the team, Jess walks off the football field alongside the coach, Joe, their shoulders brushing together as they move briskly towards the viewer front-on. From this point of view, the scene invites maximum audience involvement. We are directly challenged at this early stage to make meaning of the coach–athlete encounter as that which produces excess, a certain something, a tacit recognition of a possibility suggested if not articulated. Indeed, for a first meeting it is somewhat surprising that coach and athlete are in such close physical proximity, the early contact suggesting ease and possible mutual attraction. The ambiguity of the scene is reinforced by Joe being considerably taller than Jess, the image producing a stark sense of visual *inequality*. Thus, Joe's height differential can be interpreted as a representation of his symbolic power, coach over athlete. This opens the possibility of questioning the potential for future impropriety and exploitation on the one hand, or moral probity on the other. Either way, such difference invokes a certain "representational metafunction" (Halliday, 1978; Kress & van Leeuwen, 1996), affirming the power and masculinity of the male coach to initiate either a process of becoming more involved with or remaining detached from a less powerful yet apparently willing female subject. As they move off the field a dialogue ensues, with Joe peering down at Jess:

Joe: "How did it feel out there?"

Jess: "Brilliant, really, really great".

Joe: "I've never seen an Indian girl into football".

Jess: "I didn't even know they had a girls' team here".

At this salient moment, looking to the left of screen Joe provocatively points outwards and with a sparkle in his eye, chants: "It's all her fault, I used to play for the men's club". The striking figure of Jules, a similar height to Joe, enters the frame from the left and without breaking stride joins the pair, the three now walking abreast as they proceed off field and towards the camera.

In a practiced way, barely pausing, Joe opens a holdall for Jules to drop two footballs. He continues: "She used to hang around here whining there's no team for her to play on". Jules' mouth drops open in playful astonishment at this; a smile envelops an enticing gaze, glances cut across Jess, a shorter and marginalised yet central figure. Visually, the scene produces a powerful representational and compositional function: Joe and Jules flanking Jess and talking above (or indeed over) her head, almost as parental figures. The apparent visual chemistry is symbolically produced by a compelling line or vector (Jewitt & Oyama, 2001) running transactively between the lateral gaze and interaction of the two flanking characters. As onlookers, we are drawn to this and cannot evade its seduction; the spatial syntax producing an irresistible symmetry and equality of familiarity between coach and athlete, reinforced through the narrative.

"Whoahhh! I wasn't whining" retorts Jules, she and Joe now unreservedly laughing in an overtly flirtatious way, their bodies symmetrically aligned, matching stride for stride and arms swinging in harmony. Shifting her gaze down towards Jess, whose lowered head conceals a discrete smile, Jules continues: "Nah, there was nothing here for us girls, I mean there was junior boys stuff, but when he busted his knee (briefly touching her mouth before folding her arms and picking up Joe's attention) he set up a girls' side and he's been on my case ever since". Glancing at Jess to capture her interest, Joe addresses Jules full-on, chortling: "You see they made me start at the bottom; you can't get much lower than her". Again, Jules' mouth drops open with feigned incredulity matched with spontaneous laughter. She retorts: "You're full of it!" and retreats in an apparently coy manner, looking down, arms folded, pretending to be hurt. She continues, "Nah, we get as many trophies as the men do". Joe's gaze now shifts to engage Jess. Her head remains lowered in an attempt to conceal her amusement and perhaps partial embarrassment, as an interloper spoiling a possibly improper over-familiarity between Joe and Jules. Then another salient moment arises, when Jules puts her arm around Jess's shoulder and abruptly pulls her to one side, left of screen and away from Joe. The girls are in profile, turned obliquely away from the audience and facing their coach. Jules asks: "So, does she pass?" Jules and Joe now fix their gaze downwards on Jess who looks hopefully towards Joe.

Joe: "Are your folks up for it?"

Jess: "Yeah they're cool".

Joe: "I suppose you'd better come back then! I've gotta go up in the bar and do some real work".

He playfully punches out towards Jules, making contact with her left shoulder and forcing it back on impact, before swiftly departing off screen to the right. The salience of the "punch" frames a telling discontinuity: the portrayal of a different sort of physicality, more symbolically brutal. The "incident" both reasserts Joe's power as a male coach and simultaneously portrays a notion of hegemonic masculinity to displace Jules as a romantic possibility and construct her as "one of the boys".

Jules stands smirking and tilting her head to one side, admiring her coach as he moves away:

Jules: "He likes you".

Jess: "Do you think so?"

Jules: "He asked you back didn't he?"

The scene continues with Jules and Jess discussing football, the tone shifting in Joe's absence.

Selection two

Later in the film, following a practise session one evening, the young women leave the clubhouse by the top exit and descend the outside stairs. Jules is the last to leave, but turns quite suddenly and with her back to the audience embraces Joe who is standing, overseeing the players' departure. She places her arms around his neck and mutters something that we cannot quite hear but which conveys a semblance of intimacy. Despite the display of earlier friendliness and/or explicit flirtation captured in selection one, Joe appears not to reciprocate but instead stands motionless, almost statuesque with hands behind his back looking dismissively away from camera. Whilst not uttering a word, his body language strongly suggests the need to create physical distance between himself and Jules. This is a salient moment in terms of sensory modality (Kress & van Leeuwen, 1996), of a "point of view" that is highly "naturalistic". It conveys a suggestion that it would be quite inappropriate to reciprocate Jules' intimate embrace and makes a symbolic appeal to a broader intertextual convention, that intimate relations and touch are inappropriate in coach–athlete relationships. Thus, while at one level Joe's behaviour can be interpreted as an odd reaction given the earlier analysis, a different view of his reticence connects with the intertextual influence of self-policing (Piper et al., 2012) enacted in the presence of other team members. In the previous selection, shared intimacy between coach and athletes was constructed as a semi-private encounter, but here it is exhibited publicly. Accordingly, the coach can be seen to be governed (Foucault, 1979) by the "conduct of conducts" in which personal desires defer to professional responsibilities and hence the reaffirmation of a formal division and distance between coach and athlete.

Selection three

This ambiguity is further compounded within the same visual assemblage through immediately cutting to a different scene. Here, Joe can be observed officiating behind Jess and Jules who are performing a practise drill. The young women are chasing a ball moving directly on a path towards the audience a visual framing that beckons attention. The drill is repeated visually several times; on the last occasion Joe appears to tease and/or deliberately provoke the women, who in turn bring him to the ground, smother him and playfully punch him, Joe feigning helplessness. The symbolic juxtaposition of inappropriate touching noted earlier with counter examples of acceptable physical contact serve to frame an intriguing moral ambiguity: that the practice of touching, of what constitutes appropriate and inappropriate touch, is simultaneously continuous and discontinuous. This point is illustrated later at a bus stop, Jules and Jess framed in profile laughing together; Jess pops a question: "Jules, you know Joe, do you like him?" Shrugging, turning away and pretending to be somewhat embarrassed, Jules replies: "Nah, he'd get sacked if he was caught shagging one of his players".

Jess: "Really?"

Jules: "Sometimes I wish I could find a bloke just like him though, you know, that wasn't off limits ..."

Jess: "I hope I end up marrying an Indian boy like him too" Jules bursts out laughing and doubles over ...

Jess: "Shut up!!"

This dialogue is pertinent in reinforcing Jules' desire to be sexually intimate with Joe. Yet by skilfully evading the question of whether she actually likes him, she instead takes responsibility and projects a generalised moral imperative (Jewitt & Oyama, 2001) that all coaches should be mindful of moral and professional responsibilities in relation to their athletes. In Foucauldian terms (1977; 1979), the nature of the disciplinary technology (and hence imputed notion of moral probity) constructs a field of action by putting in place the possible outcome: the potential loss of employment and career. While recognising that Joe is "off limits", both young women still appear infatuated with him, or at least the symbolic image of the role he discharges; Jules wishes she could "find a bloke just like him" and Jess hopes to "end up marrying an Indian boy like him too". This joint confession produces a salience (Kress & van Leeuwen, 1996) that re-emerges in later scenes.

Selection four

A development in the plot is that Jess's parents, with traditional notions of propriety, are not happy with her playing football and finally forbid it. A further contradiction and discontinuity arises during a club trip to play in Germany. One evening Joe and the team are waiting outside their hotel lobby for a taxi to a nightclub. Jess (who has travelled with the team but is believed by her parents to be staying with relatives in London) makes an appearance in a stunning black dress (having been dressed for the part by Jules), enjoying attention. Distracted by the rest of the team, Joe is then alerted to her entrance; the camera moves in on his face as he looks Jess up and down, admiring her and perhaps even metaphorically touching her as a sexual object before shaking the trance and reinforcing the call for a taxi. At the nightclub, Jules beckons Joe to dance several times but Joe refuses and remains steadfast until finally conceding to pressure. The two link hands on the dance floor, moving and touching provocatively, perhaps even inappropriately given the contradictory imperative. Shortly, Joe approaches Jess and invites her to join in the dancing. He holds the hands of both young women as they all dance together, but eventually lets go of Jules to pay Jess more attention. Feeling the effect of alcohol, Jess holds her head and motions to exit the nightclub with Joe quickly following. Outside on the rooftop Jess stumbles but is saved by Joe who puts his arms around her shoulder and waist, bringing her in close to his side and asking if she is alright. Declaring that she had only a couple of glasses of wine, Jess perches against a wall before complaining about her head and the smoke inside. The two are now in very close proximity, Joe peering down on Jess in a manner that is almost predatory. A dialogue ensues, referring back to an earlier scene where Joe had intervened on behalf of Jess with her parents, attempting to allay their fears regarding her footballing ambitions.

Jess: "That was so brilliant the way you came to my house. You were brave enough to face my mum. Your dad can't be as mad as her". Joe retorts: "Your mam's a barrel of laughs compared to my dad".

Stroking Jess's hair Joe continues: "I don't need to feel close to my family Jess. I don't need you to feel sorry for me".

The scene then cuts to Jules who has arrived outside and is looking positively horrified. Joe and Jess move closer oblivious to Jules' covert presence. Looking into each other's eyes, it is Jess that makes the first move, motioning forward to attempt a kiss with Joe before Jules intervenes shouting "you bitch". The kiss is thwarted and Jess and Joe are left feeling awkward with Jules storming back inside the nightclub.

The salience of this scene is contained in the way that all three characters can be seen to transgress the generalised moral imperative noted earlier, by disregarding the professional distance expected between coach and athlete. Indeed it appears that, away from the immediate context of football, coach–athlete boundaries are reciprocally relaxed. Tellingly, the young women are both 18 years of age and therefore technically adults who are able to make their own judgements concerning what counts as appropriate and inappropriate behaviour. Even so, moral ambiguity prevails in terms of the nature, role and salience of intertextuality. Some observers (Brackenridge, 2001 and others) argue from the "point of view" of Kant's categorical imperative (Acton, 1970), that irrespective of particular circumstances it is de facto always wrong for a professional in a position of power and responsibility to become intimately involved with an athlete; to ignore the imperative would constitute a breach of conduct and possible sexual exploitation. However, in this view the athlete is always positioned as subordinate in the relationship and conceived as vulnerable; assumptions which can be strongly questioned on many levels (Johansson, 2013).

Selection five

This point is especially resonant given the perspective of the young women, as symbolically represented several scenes later. Following a rift between the two women over the nightclub "incident", Jess visits Jules at home. There is a frosty atmosphere between them and Jess's face appears full of fear and trepidation as she anticipates delivering an apology.

Jess: "Look Jules I feel really bad about what happened".

Jules: "Yeah well you should", turning her head away and to profile in disapproval.

Jess: "I'm sorry, I don't want you to be in a strop with me".

Looking directly at the audience to engage our judgement, Jules retorts: "I'm not in a strop"

Jess: "But it was a mistake, I didn't know what I was doing".

Jules looks on with venom and disgust: "I can't believe you kissed him".

Jess, looking somewhat confused: "I didn't".

Jules: "Yeah right, Jess I know what I saw, you knew he was off-limits … don't pretend to be so innocent – you knew exactly how I felt about him".

Jess: "You told me you didn't even like him, now you're acting as though you're in love with him".

Jules: "You don't know the meaning of love. You've really hurt me Jess. That's all there is to it, you've betrayed me".

Jess: "So that's it?"

Jules: "Yeah, that's it. Bye!"

In this encounter it is interesting that Jules once again employs the expression "off-limits" in relation to Joe. Previously, she had used it to suggest he was unobtainable precisely because he is the coach. Now, however, the meaning is subverted to suggest that he is not so much "off-limits" as to be unavailable to Jess, since Jules tacitly discloses she is also infatuated with Joe – "you knew exactly how I felt about him". As a mode of representation the scene has high modality (Jewitt & Oyama, 2001). Jules' facial expression is replete with sorrow and woe, which despite her tacit admission produces an "effect of power", which potentially draws the audience into her narrative and thus onto her side. Moreover, the discursive slippage serves to underscore the point that none of the central characters is able to fully maintain a consistent moral line throughout the film, which contributes to its ambiguity. This point is supported in our final extract in which Joe, in the aftermath of the nightclub debacle, articulates a stricter professional line.

Selection six

Following an incident during a tournament match where Jess is fouled by an opponent and her shirt torn, she becomes involved in an altercation with the offending player, who calls her a "Pakki". The two players end up pushing each other and this results in Jess being sent off for violent conduct, the referee not having heard the racist abuse. In the changing room after the match, Joe admonishes Jess, shouting while aggressively pointing in her face: "What the hell's wrong with you? I don't wanna see anything like that from you ever again. Do you hear me? We're lucky they're not suspending players in this tournament". At this point, he turns to commend and applaud the rest of the team for their win and performance, before sharply exiting the changing room. Jess storms out after him: "Why did you yell at me like that? You knew the ref was out of order". Joe continues to walk away dismissively with Jess in pursuit. Turning and fiercely pointing, Joe snaps: "You could have cost us the tournament!" Jess, becoming tearful, replies: "It wasn't my fault, you didn't have to shout at me". Facing Jess front on, both now in profile to the audience, Joe emphatically states: "I am your coach, I have to treat you the same as everyone else". Holding out his hands in front of her, in a plea for empathy while looking passionately into her eyes, he continues: "Look Jess I saw what happened, she fouled you, she tugged your shirt, you just over-reacted that's all". Jess: "It's not all. She called me a Pakki, but I guess you wouldn't understand what that feels like, would you?" Holding both hands to his chest Joe sighs: "Oh yes, I'm Irish. Of course I understand what that feels like". Then, putting both hands on Jess's shoulders, he pulls her to an intimate embrace, her nose pressed closely into his chest while fighting back tears.

Quite how we, the audience, are supposed to reconcile Joe's claim to treat Jess the same as everyone else, while only moments later pulling her to an intimate embrace, presents an intriguing negative and moral quandary. The obvious contradiction is symbolic of the ambiguous tone throughout, producing corollary implications for the way in which relationships between coaches and athletes both reflect and construct meaning in real-life situations.

Conclusion

After a successful end to the season, the film concludes with the reconciled Jess and Jules being selected for football scholarships at a university in the U.S., a key step towards a professional career; Jess's parents have accepted her choice and intention. Jess and Joe admit to each other they are romantically involved and plan to confront Jess's parents with this when she returns at Christmas. Thus, in 2002 the cinematic conventions of a feel-good romantic comedy, with a happy ending, were met. It is no criticism of the film to note that the tensions and contradictions around touch and intimacy, on which the narrative had played, and which we have sought to explore, are left unresolved or simply avoided. Significantly, the burgeoning relationship between Joe and Jess is permitted only once she has moved on and he has ceased to be her coach. In previous decades this may have seemed less of an issue, with high-profile female athletes marrying their coaches (Jackie Joyner in 1986, Isabelle Duchesnay in 1991, Paula Radcliffe in 2001). However, by the time the film was released, for a coach–athlete relationship to reach that stage would have required the contravention of significant guidelines on appropriate behaviour and socio-physical distance, and would have attracted negative responses and possible sanction. Although intimate relations between coach and athletes above the age of consent are not prohibited in law, they are effectively forbidden in many sports. Olympic champion cyclist Victoria Pendleton risked her relationship with her governing body when, aged 27, she courted and married her coach, and suffered hostility (McRae & Pendleton, 2012). Extreme anxiety around child abuse has extended into even adult athlete–coach relationships, and while rationalisations for this proscriptive approach are offered (e.g. power imbalances, age differences, contrary responsibilities), the process is based on the infantilisation of the athletes (usually women) who cannot be trusted with agency and are always considered victims.

Viewing the film in 2015 following the implementation of draconian "no touching" and "no relationship" guidelines by sports governing bodies, we see it through a different lens. In spite of the suggestion that it avoids confronting the tensions and contradictions it portrays, it remains notable that it shows the coach–athlete relationship as human and normal. Joe is not an automaton; his performance varies over time and between contexts, and his athletes respond in human ways. Indeed, were the film to be produced today it might be condemned as irresponsible by the CPSU and others, as Joe acts in ways which today would be considered to be evidence of "grooming". Thus, he would be seen as dangerous, improper and punishable. However, here is a coach who seems to put the well-being and development of his charges before self-protection. When Jess is unwilling to be seen in shorts (for cultural reasons and because her knee is scarred from a childhood accident with fire) Joe sits alone in the stand with her and compares her burn marks with his own heavily scarred post-operative knee. Later, when she appears to have sprained an ankle, alone on the edge of the field he removes her sock and manipulates her foot. Both actions would cause apoplexy today; he is alone, unwitnessed and risks allegations of abuse. Yet in the film, the characters carry these events off in a relatively relaxed way; the coach is acting like a coach and, whatever might happen away from the training ground, it is accepted as normal and positive. In this sense, watching *Bend it Like Beckham* offers a reminder of a world which we have lost but that, with some clearer thinking and good sense, we may choose to find again.

Disclosure statement

No potential conflict of interest was reported by the authors.

References

Acton, H. B. (1970). *Kant's moral philosophy*. London: Macmillan.
Bach, P., & Tipper, S. P. (2006). Bend it like Beckham: Embodying the motor skills of famous athletes. *The Quarterly Journal of Experimental Psychology, 59*, 2033–2039.
Barthes, R. (1977). Rhetoric of the image. In R. Barthes (Ed.), *Image – Music – Text*. (R. Barthes, Trans.) S. Heath (pp. 32–51). New York, NY: Hill and Wang.
Brackenridge, C. (2001). *Spoilsports*. London: Routledge.
Caudwell, J. (2009). *Girlfight* and *Bend it Like Beckham*: Screening women, sport, and sexuality. *Journal of Lesbian Studies, 13*, 255–271.
Cohen, S. (1999). Moral panics and folk concepts. *Paedagogica Historica, 35*, 585–591.
Department of Health. (1999). *Working together to safeguard children*. London: The Stationery Office.
Donnell, A. (2007). Feeling good? Look again! Feel good movies and the vanishing points of liberation in Deepa Mehta's *Fire* And Gurinder Chadha's *Bend It Like Beckham*. *Journal of Creative Communications, 2*, 43–55.
Foucault, M. (1979). *Governmentality. Ideology and Consciousness, 6*, 5–21.
Foucault, M. (1980). Truth and power. In C. Gordon (Ed.), *Power/knowledge: Selected interviews and other writings 1972–1977* (pp. 109–133). London: Tavistock.

Foucault, M. (1983). Afterword, the subject and power. In H. L. Dreyfus & P. Rabinow (Eds.), *Michel foucault: Beyond structuralism and hermeneutics* (2nd ed., pp. 208–226). Chicago, IL: University of Chicago Press.

Foucault, M. (1991). On the genealogy of ethics: An overview of work in progress. In P. Rabinow (Ed.), *The Foucault reader* (pp. 340–372). London: Penguin.

Foucault, M. (2002a). Truth and juridical forms. In J. D. Faublon (Ed.), *Michel foucault – Power volume 3 – The essential works of foucault 1954–1984* (pp. 1–89). London: Penguin.

Foucault, M. (2002b). *Archaeology of Knowledge*. London: Routledge.

Furedi, F. (2002). *Culture of fear*. London: Continuum.

Garratt, D., & Piper, H. (2014). Dangerous liaisons: Youth sport, citizenship and intergenerational mistrust. *International Journal of Sport Policy and Politics*. Retrieved from http://dx.doi.org/10.1080/19406940.2014.8963901-14

Garratt, D., Piper, H., & Taylor, B. (2013). 'Safeguarding' sports coaching: Foucault, genealogy and critique. *Sport, Education and Society, 18*, 615–629.

Giardina, M. D. (2003). "Bending it like Beckham" in the global popular – Stylish hybridity, performativity, and the politics of representation. *Journal of Sport and Social Issues, 27*, 65–82.

Gibson, J. J. (1979). *The ecological approach to visual perception*. Boston, MA: Houghton Mifflin.

Halliday, M. A. K. (1978). *Language as social semiotic*. London: Edward Arnold.

Jewitt, C., & Oyama, R. (2001). Visual meaning: A social semiotic approach. In T. van Leeuwen & C. Jewitt (Eds.), *Handbook of visual analysis* (pp. 134–156). London: Sage.

Johansson, S. (2013). Coach-athlete sexual relationships: If no means no does yes mean yes? *Sport, Education and Society, 18*, 678–693.

Kress, G., & van Leeuwen, T. (1996). *Reading images: The grammar of visual design*. London: Routledge.

Kvale, S. (2008). *Doing interviews*. London: Sage.

McRae, D., & Pendleton, V. (2012). *Between the lines: My autobiography*. London: HarperCollins.

Piper, H. (2014). Touch, fear, and child protection – Immoral panic and crusade. *Power & Education, 6*, 229–240.

Piper, H., Garratt, D., & Taylor, B. (2013). Child abuse, child protection, and defensive 'touch' in PE teaching and sports coaching. *Sport Education and Society, 18*, 583–598.

Piper, H., & Garratt, D. (2012). Hands off sports coaching: the politics of touch, RES000-22-4156. Final report prepared for the Economic and Social Research Council. Swindon: ESRC.

Piper, H., Taylor, B., & Garratt, D. (2012). Sports coaching in risk society: No touch! No trust! *Sport, Education and Society, 17*, 331–345.

Ratna, A. (2011). 'Who wants to make aloo gobi when you can bend it like Beckham?' British Asian females and their racialised experiences of gender and identity in women's football. *Soccer and Society, 12*, 382–401.

Roy, A. G. (2006). Translating difference in *Bend it Like Beckham*. *New Cinemas: Journal of Contemporary Film, 4*, 55–66.

Taylor, B., Piper, H., & Garratt, D. (2014). Sports coaches as 'dangerous individuals' – Practice as governmentality. *Sport Education and Society*. Retrieved from http://www.tandfonline.com/doi/full/10.1080/13573322.2014.8994921-17

The Stationery Office. (1996a). *Childhood matters: Report of the national commission of inquiry into the prevention of child abuse: Volume 1: The report*. London: Author.

The Stationery Office. (1996b). *Childhood matters: Report of the national commission of inquiry into the prevention of child abuse: Volume 2: Background papers*. London: Author.

'We're In This Together:' neoliberalism and the disruption of the coach/athlete hierarchy in CrossFit

Leslie Heywood

Department of English, Binghamton University – State University of New York (SUNY), Binghamton, NY, USA

ABSTRACT

CrossFit is a growing model of fitness that defines itself in opposition to conventional fitness practices. "Specializing in not specializing", CrossFit aims to provide a General Physical Preparedness programme sustainable and scalable across an athlete's life course. "Fitness" is achievable through "constantly varied high intensity functional movements performed across broad time and modal domains". A differential modality of time is operational in CrossFit, which includes the "clock time" of earlier eras but is largely characterised by the "network time" that makes CrossFit omnipresent. Characterised by the neoliberal rhetoric of self-improvement and individual responsibility, CrossFit takes these ideas one step further by extending its practice and philosophy to every aspect of an athlete's life, including their network of personal relationships. CrossFit's lack of specialisation and articulation within network time function to shift the role of the coach from central authority to one who performs affective, emotional labour and forms of a "relationship" that involves supporting each individual athlete in the achievement of their own goals inside and outside "the box".

I. "What is CrossFit?": CrossFit's Oppositional Stance

CrossFit, a sport and training method that combines many sport disciplines, has a motto that declares, "we specialize in not specializing" (Glassman, 2013). For instance, athletes at the CrossFit Games never know until the night before what the next day's events will be. "We force you to train a holistic package", Games Director Dave Castro says. "You can't prepare for these things ... you prepare in trying everything" (Cannon & Glancy, 2014). The "prepared for everything" modality relies on a fundamental decentralisation of the usual sport preparation paradigm, which is to be as focused and specialised as possible at one sport. But CrossFit combines tests across every domain of physical activity, from running to swimming to gymnastics to Olympic lifting to log carrying. As a result, no one coach can prepare the athlete for everything, and many athletes rely on remote coaching. In this form of coaching, a coach will write individual programming for a specific athlete and send it to them, and the athlete relies on videos taken of their sessions for feedback along with performance measures like the time it took to complete a task.

Because it comes from a different model and set of assumptions than those of mainstream fitness, and because CrossFit is the name for both a particular model of fitness training and is the "Sport of Fitness" in its own right, there is a great deal of confusion about what, exactly, CrossFit is. As a training method it is "for everyone", but as a sport, the CrossFit Games claims to produce "the fittest men and women on the planet". In its "About" section, the CrossFit Games' home page states that the CrossFit Games "are the world's premier test to find the Fittest on Earth™. They are world-renowned as a grueling test for the world's toughest athletes and 'one of the fastest growing sports in America,' according to *Forbes*" (http://games.crossfit.com/about-the-games, retrieved 7 January 2016).

The Games as a sport at least partly claims to be "premiere" because it defines itself in opposition to mainstream sports:

> The Games were created to fill a void – no other true test of fitness existed ... Even decathlons, while testing a relatively wide range of abilities, missed vital components of physical fitness. The Games events are made up of a broad range of functional movements [that] move large loads, long distances, quickly. These movements also form the basis of our exercise program ... ("About the Games," http://games.crossfit.com/about-the-games, retrieved 7 January 2016).

CrossFit's training platform is formulated similarly. It defines "fitness" as "your ability to move large loads, long distances, quickly, in the broadest variety of domains", and claims "the ability to sustain that fitness throughout your life is a defining measure of health. CrossFit's prescription for achieving this fitness is constantly varied high intensity functional movements. We can accurately predict improvements in work capacity across broad time, modal, and age domains through this prescription" (http://journal.crossfit.com/2009/02/crossfits-new-definition-of-fitness-volume-under-the-curve-2.tpl, retrieved 15 December 2015). In this model, the specialisation characteristic of the usual sports that measure ability in only one particular area is the very thing CrossFit defines itself against. Therefore, the "fittest" must be good at everything, not just one thing such as throwing a ball or even multiple things such as running, swimming and biking like in triathlons.

Partly due to the lack of specialisation, and therefore a lesser reliance on a single coaches' authority, in CrossFit we can see a transformational paradigm emerging in which the usual coach/athlete hierarchy is disrupted. While there has been a shift away from the authoritative coaching model overall, this shift is particularly emphasised in CrossFit. Craig Stewart notes in "The Negative Behaviors of Coaches" that a current focus within coach education is "the identification of good behaviors [of coaches] and the elimination of bad behaviors" (Stewart, 2013, p. 8). Stewart's analysis of 10 years worth of samples from students in introductory coaching classes that described the best and the worst behaviours of coaches in their athletic experiences correlated the worst behaviours with too much power and authority: "authoritarian, power trip, dictator, arrogant, conceited, self-centered, egotistical, cocky", while good behaviours correlated with themes like "caring, compassion, and communication" (Stewart, 2013, p. 7). So while the larger coaching community advocates a less authoritarian style as well, in CrossFit, due to the decentralised authority, emphasis on community and individual athletes working with multiple coaches, the shift is a product of the form of the practice as well as its function (Belger, 2012; Herz, 2014).

In Crossfit, there are a few revered coaches who specialise in one area such as Mike Burgener for Olympic Lifting, and these coaches travel worldwide giving Specialty Certifications in these areas, but the actual coaches Games athletes work with are most often other athletes or some coach themselves. Furthermore, while the daily competitions that form the comparative performances of workouts (WODs) at each CrossFit box (gym) are led by a coach, that coach's role, as I will analyse later, is more one of affective support even though he/she is also supposed to have the practical information the athlete needs. Within this shift away from the figure of the coach as a centralised authority, within CrossFit culture, simultaneously everyone is an authority, and no one is. I will argue that there is a link between this more horizontal relationship between coach and athlete and the training modalities such as remote programming and video analysis, and that CrossFit represents a shift in the sporting paradigm away from dependence on a coach to at least the illusion of self-reliance. This shift is framed by a larger cultural shift away from "clock time" – the present of the workout and its timed outcomes to the all-encompassing nature of "networked time" ("digitally compressed clock time") as well (Hassan, 2003, p. 233). This shift is imbricated within CrossFit founder Greg Glassman's libertarian leanings, where an emphasis on self-making tends to mask an adherence to a very specific ideology of production and self-production that is "on at all times" and that is part of the CrossFit vision.

II. CrossFit in a neoliberal/libertarian frame

As in the sport nexus more generally, representations of sport coaching in CrossFit should be located specifically in the context of neoliberalism. As Michael L. Silk and David L. Andrews discuss in "Sport and the Neoliberal Conjuncture", neoliberalism provides an identificatory framework to illuminate "the practices, policies, and processes responsible for the normalization of neoliberal sporting cultures" (Silk & Andrews, 2012, p. 15). "Neoliberalism" is the name generally given to a dominant twenty-first century economic paradigm, and marks a particular stance towards globalisation often referred to as the "Washington consensus". It is a set of assumptions that is used to shape policy, and necessarily has an effect on the cultural practices that occur within its context (Held & McGrew, 2003). The neo-liberalism of the Washington consensus advocates "deregulation, privatization, structural adjustment programs, and limited government" (Held & McGrew, 2003, p. 5). It has been framed succinctly by postcolonial scholars Munshi and Willse (2015):

> We understand neoliberalism as the form of capitalism that has dominated transna-tional economic systems since the early 1970s. As an ideology, neoliberalism is predi-cated upon the belief that the maximization of social good requires locating all human action in the domain of the market ... This conceptual linking of market growth and individual freedom has meant that the spread of neoliberal economic policy has come to be seen as equivalent to the spread of democracy.

These ideologies, policies, and practices are often accompanied by a reduction in public spending on social services and public goods of all kinds including roads, bridges, even fire departments, as well as a reduction in government controls pertaining to the environment and safety on the job.[1] In the neoliberal view, individual responsibility for one's own condition is paramount. While neoliber-alism seems to no longer be functioning as a seamless ideology the way it did at the end of the twentieth century, it nonetheless has had an impact on all sectors of human interaction, including sport, and is articulated within CrossFit in very particular ways.

Greg Glassman, the CEO of CrossFit, Inc. who is credited with its invention, is outspoken about his neoliberal and libertarian orientation. CrossFit, Inc. – the parent organisation of all the CrossFit affiliate boxes (which are fully independent but have to pay CrossFit Inc. a yearly affiliation fee, which ranges from $1000 to $4000 USD depending on when you affiliated) articulates a provocatively oppo-sitional stance to mainstream fitness industry, fully in alignment with the larger context of neoliberalism. Glassman calls himself a "rabid libertarian", and asserts that this philosophy – which shares the economic assumptions of neoliberalism and extends these to the social realm as well – reflects CrossFit (Glassman, 2013).[2] This philosophy reinforces a particular set of assumptions about fitness and how it should be practiced/taught.

According to Glassman (who is a former gymnast and son of a Hughes Aircraft rocket scientist), CrossFit

> delivers a fitness that is, by design, broad, general, and inclusive. Our specialty is not specializing. Combat, survival, many sports, and life reward this kind of fitness and, on average, punish the specialist. The CrossFit program is designed for universal scalabil-ity making it the perfect application for any committed individual ... We've used our same routines for elderly individuals with heart disease and cage fighters one month out from televised bouts. We scale load and intensity; we don't change programs. The needs of Olympic athletes and our grandparents differ by degree not kind. (http://www.crossfit.com/cf-info/what-crossfit.html).

Like Charles Darwin's formulation about the differences between species, "differ-ing in degree but not in kind", in this formulation CrossFit is as inevitable as and is structured similar to evolution itself – it is the evolution of fitness. WODs are infinitely scalable, so they are the same WOD built on the same principles, but only vary in weight used and reps performed, "differing from" the prescribed WOD "by degree but not in kind". CrossFit offers a supportive community in the global context of the dissolution of community, but it also promotes the "survival" of the few, those with money and leisure time enough to make CrossFit a part of their daily lives. As it does in other areas, CrossFit's oppositional stance to mainstream fitness has fundamental consequences for the role of the coach as well.

Because CrossFit is based on a coaching model where athletes come to a small class whose programme is written by certified coaches and whose movements are supervised by a coach or coaches each day, it is an intensive, hands-on model created in opposition to the anonymous pay-your-cash-and-you're-on-your-own model of the regular gyms.[3] The scale is much smaller – a given "box" can only serve a limited number of athletes. One pays for this kind of personal attention: instead of a typical $200 per year gym membership, many CrossFit boxes charge around $200 per month. The cost does seem to have an impact on CrossFit's characteristic demographic, which is largely white men and women making more than $100 K per year (McMahon, 2013). So while the coach in this model is imperative to CrossFit's success, at the same time a given box succeeds or fails on its own, and this philosophy is often passed down to the clients, who ultimately bear the responsibility for their own success for failure in CrossFit.

This is perhaps one reason why people outside the CrossFit movement often refer to it as a "cult" – CrossFit sees itself as doing nothing less than facilitating its participants' survival, training them to be always self-sufficient and engaged in constant self-improvement. Sport sociologist Marcelle C. Dawson identifies CrossFit as a "reinventive institution" in which "power, identity construction, and self-transformation" occur in a context of "voluntarism, performative regulation, and mutual surveillance" that is in some ways antithetical to autonomy and agency Dawson, 2015, p. 1). The way CrossFit ideology expands to include all domains of a practitioner's life is openly stated as all-encompassing. "Fitness is not just in the gym, it's also outside the gym ... it's life", says Matt Chan, a multi-Games competitor and coach in many forums, from CrossFit Headquarters staff to online coaching to guest coaching at different boxes (Cannon & Glancy, 2014).

Fitness as "life", using fitness in a functional modality to be "prepared for anything", is a CrossFit cornerstone linked to what sociologist Robert Hassan calls "network time", digitally compressed clock time in which "time duration is limited only by technical capacities" (Hassan, 2003, p. 233). Partly because of its manifestations through the connectivity of the CrossFit main site with its ever-proliferating content of nutrition and performance articles, WODs, research and news, each box's own website with its daily WODs and interactive templates where box members post their daily performances, and modalities such as online coaching, CrossFit can reach into every aspect of an athlete's life – all CrossFit, all the time: network time. CrossFit's online aspects are further amplified because the challenging nature of the physical training comes with a cultural mandate for athletes to be supportive of each other within the confines of the group they are training with, so that CrossFit culture encourages the development of a "CrossFit family" that socialises with each other outside of the box (Belger, 2012). Anyone who isn't interactive with or supportive of fellow box members is reprimanded or shunned – which helps to create an atmosphere of group bonding, a sense of "us" against the world, and this tends to make CrossFit practitioners devoted to both CrossFit and their "CrossFit Fam". Indeed, as Dawson argues, "choosing to enter 'the box' suggests a sense of autonomy and agency, but upon closer inspection it is apparent that involvement in CrossFit is regulated not only by oneself, but also by the coach, and, importantly, by one's peers" (Dawson, 2015, p. 15). The omnipresent networked time of the CrossFit experience reduces the coach's distance from the athletes, and decentralises his/her authority through the mutual surveillance and norm-enforcing function performed by CrossFit peers.

This norm enforcement is important because of the way those norms claim to be oppositional to dominant sport paradigms. In an article published on the CrossFit. com website in 2008, CrossFit media relations head Russell Berger explicitly makes the connections between CrossFit's structural assumptions as a particular definition and model of fitness and the philosophy of libertarianism:

> Before you even begin CrossFit, you must choose to take a different path than the majority of your peers. You must choose to change your perspective on fitness, diet, and work. You must put in the effort as an individual to improve your ability. You must acknowledge your own responsibility to do the exercises correctly and safely. When you fail, it is no one's fault but your own. When your diet starts to slip, it is no one's fault but your own. You rely on yourself for your effort, your results, and your initiative. If an ideological affiliation had to be applied to CrossFit, it would almost certainly be the "Libertarian method" of fitness. Individual responsibility reigns, and everyone is held to the same standards of performance. (Berger, 2008)

Berger points to a central contradiction: the individual is paramount, but is held to a standardised set of expectations, which is to be able to become proficient at a wide range of physical modalities and follow a particular diet and lifestyle.

It is unusual for this kind of explicit connection to be made by representatives of that business between a mode of training and a set of ideological assumptions. Instead, assumptions behind physical practices usually go unarticulated by their authorising institutions and are only made explicit in academic analysis. For instance, science studies sociologist Kelly Moore addresses a different set of bodily practices, particularly gendered ones, in terms of their articulation through the global formation of neoliberalism. She analyses what she calls "the emotion-world of women's 'exercise' since the 1980s" (Moore, 2012–2013). That emotional world now belongs to what she terms the "striver class" – which "includes what were formerly known as the working-to-middle classes, but who are now reconfigured and defined by their mobility aspirations ... losers stand still" (Moore, 2012–2013). Mobility is embodied in the assumption behind exercise: "morphology and all other features of the self are malleable and can be changed through calculative practices that join together in the body and the mind" (Moore, 2012–2013). Bodywork is "flexible" and infinitely varied, and exercise discourses are full of advice to "never stick to one thing" so as to avoid boredom. Such body work is "expected to be joyful" and "the labor of producing a body is turned into 'fun'" (Moore, 2012–2013).

Moore captures the open-endedness and process-oriented "network" temporality of current physical practice, where goals are present but ever-receding, infinitely deferred, when she describes a "web of embodied women at work-play, endlessly producing but never reaching a goal … the consumer-entrepreneur who is always reinvesting, seeking forms of satisfaction, looking for opportunities" (Moore, 2012–2013). Sport sociologists Myra S. Washington and Megan Economides analyse the same narrative at work specifically in CrossFit: "the narrative of CF relied on some of the flawed notions that undergird postfeminist ideologies, such as empowerment through choice, neoliberalism, and meritocracy" (Washington & Economides, 2016. p. 143). I will examine CrossFit's participation in the neoliberal dictates of "flexibility", "constant variation", continual work, and "fun", the work of self-production that never stops, dictates within which the coach becomes the facilitator who provides the affective labour of support.

"Flexibility" and "fun" are two CrossFit cornerstones. Because CrossFit is a programme that is reliant on continuous variation of exercises and repetition schemes, it is a "general physical preparedness" (GPP) kind of training whose camaraderie and back-to-the-playground mentality (movements include things like jump roping, rope climbing, box jumping and monkey bars swinging, which most people haven't done since childhood) serves particular emotional needs, such as the need for adults to "play" in the context of demanding work lives where, because of information technologies, they are now always on call. If CrossFit seems to provide a safe environment where individual efforts are supported by the group, it is also directly in alignment with neoliberal principles of deregulation and non-interference. It is a physical practice in which flexibility and variation are deployed in service of larger norms, the individual forged through an intense and infinitely ongoing encounter with obstacles – the "WOD" (workout of the day, whatever that happens to be) from which one emerges victorious each time. Characteristic of the historical present in that it articulates a rhetoric of safety and flexibility simultaneously, it is, perhaps, the ideal neoliberal body practice.

III. Representing coaches in CrossFit: self-reliance, emotional labour and the erosion of coaching authority

Decentralisation, flexibility, self-reliance: these ideas combine within the culture of CrossFit to make the coach's role less important. This decentralisation and proliferation of fitness goals is reflected in the CrossFit Documentaries *Every Second Counts* (2009) and *The Test of Fitness*, the only existing films about the sport of CrossFit. The first documentary was made about the inaugural Games that were held in 2007, three years before Reebok began its official sponsorship and CrossFit became mainstream. It is important that there are a few representations of coaching in the earlier documentary, but the later one, about the 2013 Games, contains none at all. In the first documentary, the figure of the coach is merged with the athlete, so in many scenes, the athletes are speaking as coaches and vice versa. Contrary to traditional representations of coaches and athletes where the two exist in different worlds, in CrossFit most often coaches and athletes are sharing both functions, and by the second documentary, the figure of the Coach had become so incidental that there was not a single scene of an athlete being coached.

In *The Test of Fitness,* Glassman's voice resonates through the opening scene saying "more than just a competition of athletes, this is a competition of training methodologies". The "specializing in not specializing" that is the CrossFit trademark discussed earlier is paramount in the documentary. "We like to introduce elements you can't practice in a gym", head Games programmer Dave Castro says. "It's more than just a competition of the fittest alive – it's performing arts". "We're not testing specialization, we're not testing pregame strategy – we're testing in the field performance, how you respond to something you haven't trained before … we force you to train everything … some people crack under that", Games competitor and coach Matt Chan says in the documentary. Five-year Games champion Rich Froning Jr explains that "we can't anticipate the events in life, we can't anticipate what's going to happen next so we do everything we can do to be ready for what is thrown at us … that's how I train". Like the flexibility and adaptability requirements of a neoliberal economic model, CrossFit as both a fitness practice and a competitive sport requires that each individual be able to deal with whatever is thrown at them at whatever time, which again is linked to a "networked" sense of time in which CrossFit ideology and demands are omnipresent.

Representations of coaching in CrossFit are complicated, then, by the extreme decentralised nature of the training, and it is perhaps that decentralisation that accounts for the invisibility of coaches in media about the Games. As previously mentioned, an "anything goes" model of postmodern pastiche characterises coaching in CrossFit. If you're a competitive athlete, there are many online programmes you can pay for that will give you individual programming, or you can work with one particular coach (usually a Games athlete). If the local box where you train has a former or current Games athlete coaching, that box will often offer "competitor's class" in addition to the regular CrossFit classes, a class that follows harder programming and is broken up into two or even three or four workout sessions a day. For CrossFitters who aren't competing in the Games or are just competing at the local level (many CrossFit boxes will hold local or regional competitions throughout the year), you work with whoever is coaching at the time you show up to the box. Coaches often develop their own followings, but this is constrained by the variability of people's schedules and their changing needs as they progress through CrossFit.

Perhaps the one piece of media that most explicitly comments of the role of the coach in CrossFit – at the everyday, non-competitive level, anyway – is a commercial produced by CrossFit.com that ran during the 2014 CrossFit Games. "Dear Coach", a woman's voiceover says, "thank you for always being there", while the male coach – a mesomorphic baseball-capped square of a man in his late twenties or early thirties opens the obligatory garage door of the typical CrossFit box, and walks alone through the quiet of the empty box preparing for the crowd to come in. "Thank you for running a class at 5:30 in the morning so I can get home before my kids wake up", she says, as he is shown writing the WOD (workout of the day) on the whiteboard, then greeting everyone coming through the door with a high five. The group of CrossFitters shows a range of somatotypes, ranging from overweight to very thin, no one particularly muscular or intimidating, ordinary bodies. "For making sure", a male voice continues, "I build on my strengths and work on my weaknesses", as the coach adjusts a man's squat form, making sure his lower back is flat and his shoulders aren't rounded. "For being a compass that guides me to be a better version of myself", the woman continues, as the coach yells "GOOOOO!" in a general direction. "For constantly putting the needs of others before your own", the female voice continues. "For helping me lose 100 lb last year", a smiling Chicana woman says, leaning in to the coach for a hug. "For helping me realize that asthma can't stop me achieve my goals", another male voice says, in juxtaposition with a shot of a moderately fit but ordinary looking man swinging a kettlebell. "For reaffirming that life doesn't head downhill after the age of 40", another man says, in juxtaposition with more shots of men and women swinging kettlebells and doing toes to bar as the coach high fives the athletes and claps for them. "For making the impossible, possible", a female voice says, "for being an amazing coach, friend and mentor – thank you".

"Thank you for always being there", the voice continues, while the coach distributes more high fives and hugs, someone hands him a thank you note, and then he returns by himself to his office, pins the note on the bulletin board, and then stands back looking at it as the tranquil piano score ends and the CrossFit logo appears across the screen. Although clock time is present in the advertisement, the coach looks at his phone to see that it is 5:13 AM at the beginning, glances at his wrist watch later, and all the WODs are measured to the second, these specific times extend into the omnipresence of network time in which the coach's entire life has ostensibly become CrossFit and his service to his athletes not just as a coach, but also as the "friend and mentor" who is "always there".

It is striking that the advertisement undergirds the strenuous physical movements with piano rather than, as might be expected, some form of driving hard rock score. The calming sonoric environment emphasises the supportive or even soothing element of the box activity and deemphasises the physical intensity. The representation of the coach here is as a benevolent, supportive guide who is helping each athlete become "a better version of [them]selv[es]". He is a facilitator of self-improvement, a catalyst to help each athlete overcome adversity (asthma, ageing, weight issues) and complete physical tasks they didn't know they could do ("making the impossible, possible"). His most important function seems to be that he "is there", that he shows up, that he is willing to "constantly put the needs of others before his own". So although the dialogue does seem to be gendered in that it's a female voice thanking the coach for holding class "before my kids get up", and raced and gendered with the Chicana woman being the one who has needed to lose "100 lb", while male voices "build on their strengths" and women see the coach as a "compass to guide them", this representation of a coach's role seems very different from the hierarchical coach stereotype of the bald white man with a military bearing yelling out commands and calling his athletes "wusses". Here, the coach isn't so much an unquestionable authority as a facilitator, a gentle, supportive conduit through which people are inspired to "achieve their goals". The amount of affective labour he performs is highlighted by the number of shots where the coach provides actual physical gestures of support: the high fives, fist bumps, back slaps and, most importantly, the frequent hugs. This coach is physically and emotionally affectionate. A supporter, a helper, even a cheerleader, this representation of a CrossFit coach places the emphasis squarely on the athletes and the emotional labour he performs for them rather than on his all-knowing dictates.

While some of the difference from the authoritative coaching model may be accounted for by the fact that for all ostensible purposes, a CrossFit coach who isn't coaching competitive athletes seems more like a group exercise leader, this also seems to be a different model of fitness in that these ordinary athletes are doing high-skill, advanced gymnastics movements like ring dips and toes to bar, swinging heavy weights and performing highly skilled movements like Olympic lifting rather than spinning or aerobicising like traditional fitness classes do. CrossFit teaches more complicated movements, which requires a coach to have the authority/knowledge to teach those things, while it simultaneously relegates the coach to the position of affective facilitator. Teaching the skills, "making the impossible possible", is linked with the neoliberal model of continual self-improvement and striving, achieving things one didn't know one could achieve, breaking new ground, never being satisfied with the status quo or setting the bar too low. In this sense, the coach is not a centralised source of authority but rather a helper, a facilitator of individual achievement, but is paradoxically one who is not given credit for their greater knowledge or for the emotional labour they perform for each individual.

The advertisement is more than just a carefully crafted public message to sell CrossFit. It reflects the thinking of actual CrossFit coaches who have written about the coaches' role. In an article written for the *CrossFit Journal*, Ben Bergeron, one of the best-known CrossFit coaches and the head of CrossFit New England (one of the first and most successful CrossFit boxes), emphasises the importance of empathy and "connection" in producing what he calls a "great coach". "The essence of CrossFit coaching is to get our clients to move better", Bergeron writes.

But what then makes a "great coach?" I believe great coaches have the ability to go beyond the movements and connect with their athletes I call this the "deeper side of coaching," which is developing an awareness of your athletes' potential, building trust and creating an atmosphere of success The deeper side of coaching is about establishing and nurturing a strong relationship between an athlete and a coach And I would argue this relationship is the foundation of our true goals as coaches: to improve the lives, health and happiness of our clients. (Bergeron, 2011, p. 1)

For Bergeron, unlike the central authority of the traditional coach, the most important aspect of coaching is "connecting" to athletes, about "establishing and *nurturing* a strong relationship". "Nurturing" is certainly not a word that would traditionally be used to describe a coach, whose emotional distance and punitive stance were often the hallmark for "making men" of that coaches' athletes – that is, preparing them to conform to a standardised model of performance that requires self-sacrifice in many forms. In the CrossFit model, the relationship, the two-way street is paramount, because the ultimate goal is all-encompassing: the "improvement [of] the lives, health, and happiness of our clients" (Bergeron, 2011, p. 2). Bergeron quotes the course material for the Level 2 CrossFit Certification, the "Coaches Prep Course", where it says "'presence and attitude reflect your interpersonal skills. A good trainer recognizes that each person has different needs and manner in which to be dealt. It is the trainer's responsibility to determine how to relate and motivate each individual'" (Bergeron, 2011, p. 2). This emphasis draws the focus away from external performance and puts it on internal affect – how the client emotionally experiences CrossFit and internalises it as the guiding set of standards for his/her life.

This emphasis on emotional labour reflects the "customer is always right" philosophy of a decentralised liberal capital that is dependent on the continual cultivation of increasingly diversified markets to fuel growth. Understanding each athlete as an individual, and relating to them in terms of their specific needs, is a very different model than the traditional standardised model of sport where each individual athlete has to perform to a generalised norm, sacrificing their own "needs", and even health to the centralised goal of performance focused on the win. Linked to the instrumentality characteristic of the "clock time" that Hassan links in turn to the industrial era and the rise of capitalism, "that gets things done and is the dynamo that made capitalist materialism so world-conquering ... living ever more productively and efficiently" (Hassan, 2003, p. 229), the coach sees athletes instrumentally in the traditional sport model, as a means to the end achievement of winning, so that the individual athlete is only important insofar as they perform in a way that facilitates that end. There remains the residues of this in the CrossFit model and its insistence on "measurable results" that are measured in pounds and the time it takes to move them, but the more encompassing framework is that of the omnipresent, decentralised world of "networked time", that digitally compresses clock time so that there is no "time off". In this modality, articulating itself endlessly within the consumer-based dictates of CrossFit, an athlete has individual, specific goals and the focus is on them, not a larger abstraction – *because CrossFit is supposed to take over their life on every level.*

CrossFit as an all-encompassing paradigm to govern an athlete's life paradoxically articulates itself as fulfilling individual aspirations. "Observe your athletes and tailor your coaching to their personalities and goals", Bergeron writes. "Trust is the foundation of any healthy relationship, and it is vital in the coach-athlete relationship". This emphasis on relationships and trust sounds more like couples counselling that coaching norms, but Bergeron's words point to the ways that the neoliberal model has transformed the traditional coaching model to put the "client first" – because, after all, the goal is to "improve the lives, health and happiness of our clients" (Bergeron, 2011, p. 2), to transform every aspect of a client's mode of being in the world. In fact, one of Bergeron's coaching drills instructs the want-to-be-great coach that "the next time you have a conversation with someone, don't spend time preparing what you are going to say. Instead, just listen" (Bergeron, 2011, p. 4). While traditionally, it is the coach giving inspiring speeches and telling the athletes what to do, in this model, a coach is supposed to "listen", placing authority squarely with the athlete.

In its model of fitness, CrossFit is contradictory in that it is competition in the context of support, clock time in the context of networked time, individual development according to the larger context of Crossfit norms. It redefines the coach's role as one of affective, emotional labour, the formation of a "relationship" that involves supporting each individual athlete in the achievement of their own goals – whether they are competitive or not, yet at the same time, athletes are encouraged to always go beyond where they have gone before. [4] As a neoliberal, libertarian model, the individual and their individual goals take precedence over service to some larger abstraction or set of ideals, yet those "individual" goals are still in the service of the goals CrossFit establishes.

At the same time, CrossFit encourages a philosophy of accentuating only the positive, so that a given coach is supposed to "coach your next class using only the positive sense and respect the power of your words. Educate your athletes about the power of the positive and only allow for constructive thoughts and words in your gym" (Bergeron, 2011, p. 5), and "the next time someone at the gym starts gossiping about someone who isn't present, defend that person" (Bergeron, 2011, p. 4). Allowing only the positive, making sure everyone supports everyone else, turning away from a model of critical coaching where an athlete is humiliated to motivate them to perform better, coaching in CrossFit seems much more based around positive psychology than traditional coaching models, which in turn undergirds the neoliberal view that all is right in the world and athletes have to "stay positive" themselves to achieve their goals and be part of all the "positive" things going on around them.

Paradoxically, what's going on around them can encourage them to extend themselves physically in order to stay even or perform better than others in the group, so that while support of each individual is the overall philosophy, at the same time each individual needs to "bring it" every day and perform at a high level. If by chance they over-perform and push themselves beyond their own limits it is their fault and not the coach's, who is supposed to "scale" every workout to each athlete's individual needs. Symptomatic of a deregulated world where everything is supposed to sort itself out in the end, CrossFit provides a model of coaching that encourages athletes to both respect and go beyond their limits, and to recognise individual feelings and goals, while at the same time creating an atmosphere that, in Games programmer Dave Castro's words in *The Test of Fitness*, "forces people outside the margins of their experience … we know you have more than you have now". In the context of athletes training for the Games, the "always available" modality characterising network time is operational through online coaching, which allows an athlete to have multiple coaches, thus decentralising a particular coach's authority. In the context of athletes training daily at the local box, the coach becomes an affective facilitator who is "always there" for the athlete, expanding the coach's role to that of friend and member of their "CrossFit Fam", a horizontal rather than vertical relationship also informed by the omnipresence of networked time. An "individual" who "fulfills their goals" within the larger context of CrossFit norms, the athlete's emotional needs become part of the focus. As an oppositional model to the traditional fitness paradigms, CrossFit inscribes and reinscribes the role of the coach in complicated ways.

Notes

1. It is somewhat ironic, then, that CrossFit began and in many instances continues to be the training programme of choice for public institutions such as law enforcement, firefighters and the military.
2. Also see "Do Not Cross CrossFit", Inc.com, http://www.inc.com/magazine/201307/burt-helm/crossfit-empire.html.
3. CrossFit coaches are "certified" through attendance at the many Level 1 seminars hosted by CrossFit Headquarters and HQ staff (this staff often includes athletes who are or were top-level competitors in the CrossFit Games) at local boxes all over the world. You attend a two-day workshop that includes lectures and hands-on coaching, and take a test at the end of the second day. If you pass, you are "Level 1 Certified", and can coach CrossFit, ideally under the tutelage of a more experienced coach at first. There are four levels of certification, which cost $1000 USD. You have to get recertified at the Level 1 every five years at the cost of $500 USD.
4. A large majority of CrossFitters never compete. HQ encourages competing as part of the CrossFit experience, but many more CrossFitters use CrossFit as a specific way to train rather than competing in local competitions or in the various divisions of the CrossFit Games (the Open, the Regionals, and the Games – see games.crossfit.com).

Disclosure Statement

No potential conflict of interest was reported by the author.

References

Belger, A. (2012). *The power of community: CrossFit and the force of human connection*. Las Vegas, NV: Victory Belt.

Berger, R. (2008). The politics of CrossFit. *The CrossFit Journal*. Retrieved January 2, 2016, from http://library.crossfit.com/free/pdf/CFG_BergerFreedman_CrossFitPolitics-REV2.pdf

Bergeron, B. (2011). The deeper side of coaching. *The CrossFit Journal*. Retrieved January 10, 2016, from http://library.crossfit.com/free/pdf/CFJ_Coaching_Bergeron.pdf

Dawson, M. C. (2015). CrossFit: Fitness cult or reinventive institution? *International Review for the Sociology of Sport*, 1–19. http://dx.doi.org/10.1177/1012690215591793

Glassman, G. (2013). CrossFit founder greg glassman: "I'm a rabid libertarian". Retrieved January 18, 2016, from https://www.youtube.com/watch?v=-EB0XyBUl0U

Hassan, R. (2003). Network time and the new knowledge epoch. *Time and Society, 12*, 225–241.

Held, D., & McGrew, A. (Eds.). (2003). *The global transformations reader*. Cambridge: Polity Press.

Herz, J. C. (2014). *Learning to breathe fire: The rise of CrossFit and the primal future of fitness*. New York, NY: Crown Archetype.

McMahon, J. (2013). The demographics of a CrossFit box. Retrieved from http://www.jonathonmcmahon.com/1/post/2013/06/the-demographics-of-a-crossfit-box.html

Moore, K. (2012–2013). Fear and fun: Science and gender, emotion and embodiment under neoliberalism. *The Scholar and the Feminist Online, 11*. Retrieved from http://sfonline.barnard.edu/gender-justice-and-neoliberal-transformations/fear-and-fun-science-and-gender-emotion-and-embodiment-under-neoliberalism/

Munshi, S., & Willse, C. (2015). *The Scholar and the Feminist Online, 13*. Retrieved from http://sfonline.barnard.edu/navigating-neoliberalism-in-the-academy-nonprofits-and-beyond/soniya-munshi-craig-willse-introduction/#sthash.H27C2T12.dpuf

Silk, M. L., & Andrews, D. L. (2012). Sport and the neoliberal conjuncture. In M. L. Silk & D. L. Andrews (Eds.), *Sport and neoliberalism: Politics, consumption, and culture* (pp. 1–19). Philadelphia, PA: Temple University Press.

Stewart, C. (2013). The negative behaviors of coaches. *The Physical Educator, 70*, 1–14.

Washington, M. S., & Economides, M. (2016). Strong is the new sexy: Women, crossfit, and the postfeminist ideal. *Journal of Sport and Social Issues, 40*, 143–161.

Filmography

Cannon, H., & Glancy, J. (2014). *The test of fitness*. Washington, DC: CrossFit.

Matossian, S., & Peterson, C. (2009). *Every second counts*. USA: CrossFit Pictures.

Index

Note: Page number followed by n denote endnotes.

All the Right Moves 81–2
American football films 7–8, 70–2; *Any Given Sunday* 72–4; audio-visual coaching 76–8; emotionally intelligent coaching 74–6; female masculinity 78–80; wild catcalls 80–3
American professional sports, female coaches in 54
Andrews, David L. 118
Any Given Sunday 72–4
Art and Science of Gaelic football, The (O Sullivan) 19
athleticism, in women 57

Babington, Bruce 2–4
Bandealy, Ahad 7
Beckham, David 104
Bend it like Beckham 8–9, 43, 46–50, 55, 63; interpretation and moral ambiguity 106–13; overview of 104–5; rationale and conceptual frame 105–6; social semiotics 106–13
Bergeron, Ben 125–7
Berger, Russell 121
Billig, Michael 15
"bleeding chunks," of *Any Given Sunday* 73
Boone, Herman 61–2, 79
Bowman, Paul 4
Bradman, Don 14
Bronner, Simon J. 18
Brown, Terence 18

Castro, Dave 116, 123
Censorship of Films Act (1923) 16
"challenge the process" principle 32–4
Charlie's Angels 66

Chawansky, M. 64, 65
Child Protection in Sport Unit (CPSU) 106
Christy Ring 14, 16, 18, 26–7; foregrounding of Irish public in 19–20; moral authority of Catholic church in 23; première of 19–20; skill demonstration in 22–3
"Clare's Dragoons" song 22
Coach Carter 56, 57, 94
coaching films, configuring Irishness 14–27
CPSU *see* Child Protection in Sport Unit
Crawford, Scott 2
Criminal Record Bureau 106
Cronin, Mike 16–17
CrossFit: authoritative coaching model 125; coaching in 123–4; decentralisation, flexibility, self-reliance 122–3; in fitness model 127; in neoliberal/libertarian frame 118–22; nurturing in 126; oppositional stance 116–18
CrossFit Games 117, 124
Crosson, Seán 5
Cruz, Ted 5–6

Dale, Norman 30–8
D'Amato, Tony 74
Davis, Thomas Osborne 22
Dawson, Marcelle C. 120, 121
de Valera, Eamon 18, 19
Devil Wears Prada, The 66
Disclosure (1996) 64

éagrán series 17
Eddie 55, 57, 65; Coach Franklin in 63; competence in 58
emotionally abusive coach–athlete interactions 87, 88; descriptive factors of perpetrator and recipient 92–3; within educational settings 96; emotionally abusive behaviours portrayed types 93–4;

INDEX

environmental context 93; inclusion criteria for film selection 90; outcomes and responses 95; physical behaviours 97; portrayals of 89–90; reasons for use of harmful behaviours 94, 97–8; selection process 90–1; sport-related features 92; time periods 94; use of verbal behaviours 96–7
"enable others to act" principle 34–6
"encourage the heart" principle 36–7
Every Kid Can Win (Orlick & Boterill) 87

female coaches, in hollywood sports films 54–7; in American professional sports 54; authority 59–63; competence 59–63; desexualising 63–6; power 59–63; problem 57–9; respect of 59–63
Fitzgerald, Dick 18
Flying Scotsman, The 43
Forster, E.M. 2
Foucauldian genealogical approach 103
Freshman, The 81

GAA *See* Gaelic Athletic Association
Gaelic Athletic Association (GAA) 16
Gaelic games 15, 16, 18; in *Christy Ring* 20–6; Gael Linn filming 17–18; in *Peil* 20–6
Gael Linn 14, 16–19
Gellner, Ernest 15
general physical preparedness (GPP) 122
Glassman, Greg 119, 123
Goldberg, Whoopi 55
GPP *see* general physical preparedness
Gramsci, Antonio 55

Hargreaves, Jennifer 57
Hassan, Robert 120
Hawn, Goldie 59
Hayward, Susan 15, 16, 26
Hoosiers model, transformational leadership principles 5, 29–30; "challenge the process" 32–4; "enable others to act" 34–6; "encourage the heart" 36–7; "inspire a shared vision" 32–4; "model the way" 30–2
How I Play Cricket (McDonagh's) 14
How to play Gaelic football (Fitzgerald) 18
hurling game 19–22

"Inches Speech" 73, 76, 77
independent film genre 42–3
Insomnia 2

"inspire a shared vision" principle 32–4
International Framework for Coaching Excellence 44

Kerr, Gretchen 7
Kes 43
Kilmer, Bud 77, 78
Knauer, Wilhelm 79

Lemass, Seán 18
Little Girls in Pretty Boxes (Ryan) 87
Longest Yard, The 71, 79

Marcus, Louis 19
Marx, Karl 10n1
masculinity spaces 62
McDonagh, Paulette 14
McGrath, Molly 59–60, 62
Mighty Ducks, The 4
Mike Bassett 43
Minichiello, Toni 3
"model the way" principle 30–2
Montage 76
Mosse, George 56–7
motivational speech, legendary quality of 71
Mott, D. R. 19
Murray, Andy 55

National Film Institute of Ireland (NFI) 16, 17, 23
National Football League (NFL) 54
Necessary Roughness 82
North Dallas Forty 76

O'Hehir, Michael 25
Ó Móráin, Dónal 17
O Sullivan, Eamonn 18–19

Pacino, Al 73
Peil 14, 16, 18, 26–7; foregrounding of Irish public in 20–1; game footage in 25, 26; pre-match ceremony in 24–5; première of 19; skill demonstration in 21–2
Piper, Heather 8, 9
Pollock, Griselda 62
polysemy 104
professionalisation, of sport coaching 44–5
Puirseal, Padraig 19

Quarterback Princess 80, 81

Remember the Titans 61, 79, 94
Rigauer, Bruno 9

INDEX

RTÉ *see* Telefís Éireann
Ryan, Joan 87

Saroka, Phyllis 58–9, 61
Silk, Michael L. 118
Skills of Gaelic Football 19
Smith, Kathryn 54
social identity of sport coache's
    constructs 41; *Bend it like Beckham*
    46–8; critical discourse analysis
    method 45–6; ideal notion of coach
    44–5; independent film genre 42–3;
    professionalisation of sport coaching
    44–5; traditional notion of coach
    43–4; *Twenty-four seven* 48–50; types of
    knowledge 42
Sport and Irish Nationalism (Cronin) 16
Stanley, Larry 18
Stewart, Craig 117–18
Stirling, Ashley 7
Strother, B.A. 75
Sunset Park 57, 63

Telefís Éireann 17, 18
Test of Fitness, The 123, 128
"Thank You Coach" commercial 9–10
Thompson, J. 57
transformational and transactional
    leadership principles 30, 37–8; "challenge
    the process" 32–4; "enable others to
    act" 34–6; "encourage the heart" 36–7;
    "inspire a shared vision" 32–4; "model
    the way" 30–2
Twenty Four Seven 4, 43, 44, 46, 48–50

U.K. Coaching Framework 44

Varsity Blues 77–9

Washington consensus 118–19
When Saturday Comes 43, 48
Wildcats 57, 77, 79
WOD *see* workout of the day
Working Girl (1998) 64
workout of the day (WOD) 119–20, 122